Catherine Graham Bell

Managing Your Image Potential

Revised Edition

CREATING GOOD IMPRESSIONS IN BUSINESS

Prime Impressions
Kingston, Canada

Illustrations by Diane Black

Copyright © 1997, 2001 by Catherine Graham Bell

All rights reserved. First edition 1997

Revised edition 2001

No part of this book may be reproduced, transmitted in any form or by any means—electronic, mechanical, photocopying, recording or otherwise—or stored in a retrieval system, without written permission from the publisher (or in the case of photocopying or other reprographic copying, a licence from a licensing body such as the Canadian Copyright Licensing Agency), except by a reviewer, who may quote brief passages in a review.

National Library of Canada Cataloguing in Publication Data

Bell, Catherine Graham, 1951-

Managing your image potential : creating good impressions in business

Rev. ed.

ISBN 0-9682757-1-0

1. Business etiquette. 2. Clothing and dress. 3. Self-presentation.

4. Success in business. I. Title.

BJ1873.B44 2001   650.1'3   C2001-902136-4

Prime Impressions
http://www.prime-impressions.com
e-mail: catherine@prime-impressions.com

Design and illustrations: blackmac design
Editing: Stephanie Stone
Printing: Graphics Plus Printing & Advertising Inc.

Printed in Canada

Contents

Preface xiv
Acknowledgements xv
About This Book xvii

Chapter 1—Image Management Basics 1
    Creating First Impressions 1
    Communicating Visually 3
    Setting Image Management Goals 4
        SMART Goals 4
            Specific 4
            Measurable 5
            Action-Oriented 5
            Realistic 5
            Timely 6
    Using Positive Thinking 6

Chapter 2—Clothing in History 9
    As a Cultural Expression 10
    As a Social Function 10

Chapter 3—Wardrobe Strategies: Personal Criteria 13
    Recognizing Clothing Personalities 13
        Classic 14
        Dramatic 15
        Romantic 15
        Natural 15
    Lifestyle Influences 16
    Work Environment 18
    Limiting Criteria 19
        Physical Disabilities 19
        Allergies 20

Chapter 4—Your Competitive Edge:
Wardrobe Communication 23
    Dressing for Your Company Culture 23
    Dressing for the Context 24
    Dressing Down by Degrees 27
        Clothing Pieces 27
        Colour Combinations 28
        Fabric Texture and Pattern 29
        Garment Style 30
        Accessories 30
    Three Levels of Business Casual 31
        Tailored Business Casual 31
        Smart Business Casual 31
        Relaxed Business Casual 32

Chapter 5—Using Clothing Details to Your Advantage . . . 33
    Analyzing Your Body Features 34
    Lines Carry the Eye 34
    Focusing on the Face 35
    Communicating with Colour 36
    Texture Creates Illusions 38
    Pattern Balances Proportions 39

Chapter 6—Establishing a Quality Image 41
    Quality Counts 41
    Clothing Details 42
        Fads, Fashion Trends and Classics 42
        Fabric Guidelines 42
        Construction 44
        Construction Checklist 45
        Fit 47
        Fit Guidelines 47
        Exaggerated Patterns and Colours 49
        Gently Used Clothing 49

Accessories 50
    Shoes 50
    Jewellery 51
    Glasses 51
Clothing Upkeep 52
    Obvious Lack of Care 52
    Invest in a Clothes Brush and Lint Remover 53
    Jackets and Travelling 54
    Dry Cleaning 54
Personal Care 54
    Hair 55
    Fragrance 55
    Smoking Odours 56
    Personal Hygiene 56
    Fingernails 56
    Body Piercings and Tattoos 57
    Chewing and Snapping Gum 57
Physical Wellness 57
    Nutrition 57
    Physical Fitness 58
    Stress and Time Management 58

Chapter 7—Men's Image Spoilers 59
Fine-Tuning the Details 59
    Short-Sleeved Dress Shirts .59
    Tight Shirt Collars 60
    Button-Down Shirt Collars 60
    Buttoning Jackets and Vests 60
    Suit Jackets versus Blazers .61
    Overcoats 61
    Tie Tips 61
    The Wandering Waistband 64
    Stuffed Pockets 64
    Socks 65

Chapter 8—Women's Image Spoilers 67
Polish Your Professional Image 67
- Jacket Power 67
- Shoes 68
- Hosiery 68
- Skirts 69
- Pants versus Skirts 69
- Shoulder Pads 70
- Purses and Briefcases 70
- Revealing and Sleeveless Garments 70
- "Busting Out" 70
- Fabric Watch 71
- Makeup 71

Chapter 9—Planning Your Wardrobe 73
- Choosing Timeless Classics 73
  - Mixing Classics with Fashion 74
- Coordinating Textures and Patterns 74
- Taking a Closet Inventory 75
- Budgeting 77
  - Analyzing the Cost per Wearing 78
- Costing Example 78
- Building Wardrobe Modules 80
  - General Guidelines 80
- Basic Module for Men 82
  - Basic Accessories 83
- Basic Module for Women 83
  - Basic Accessories 84

Chapter 10— Fabric Characteristics and Care 87
- Natural Fibres 87
  - Cotton 87
  - Linen 88

Silk 89
Wool 89
Synthetic Fibres 90
    Acetate 91
    Acrylic 91
    Nylon 92
    Polyester 92
    Polypropylene (Olefin) 93
    Rayon/Viscose 94
Caring for and Storing Clothing 94
    Brushing and Airing Frequently 95
    Removing Stains Immediately 95
    Storing for the Season 96
    Mending Immediately 96
    Using the Correct Cleaning Method 97
    Ironing or Pressing Properly 98
    Allowing Rest Periods 98

Chapter 11—Etiquette: Method in Your Manners 99
Proper Etiquette Puts You at Ease 99
Good Manners Give You Power 100

Chapter 12—First Impressions: Making an Entrance . . .103
Standing and Moving with Confidence 103
Shaking Hands 104
    Handshake Protocol 104
Avoiding Certain Handshake Styles 106
    The Bone Crusher 106
    The Cold Fish 106
    The Two-Handed Clasp .106
    The Touchy-Feely 107
    The Arm Wrestle 107
    The Upper Hand 107

Making Eye Contact 107
Smiling 108

Chapter 13—Making Introductions **109**
    Following the Rules of Introductions 109
        Who is Introduced to Whom? 110
        Introducing Family Members 111
        Including Titles 112
        Including Last Names .112
        When Age and Rank Collide 112
        Clarifying Relationships 112
        Don't Repeat Names 113
        Don't Use "My Friend" 113
        Handling Gender 113
        Responding to an Introduction 114
    Rising When You're Being Introduced 114
    Forgetting Names 115

Chapter 14—Improving Your Business Image **117**
    Being a Responsible Person 117
    Being Reliable by Managing Your Time 118
    Handling Interruptions 118
    Respecting Everyone 119
    Creating Loyalty Inside and Outside the Company 121
    Managing Effectively 122
    Erring on the Side of Generosity 122
    Giving and Receiving Gifts 123
    Replying to Invitations 123
    Sending Notes of Thanks .124
    Practising E-Mail Etiquette 125

Chapter 15—Meeting Manners **129**
    Timing Considerations 130

Participant Involvement 130
The Agenda 131
Seating 131
The Role of the Chair 132
The Role of the Participant 133
Maximizing Your Potential 134
Making a Presentation 134
Teleconferences 135
Handling Meeting Challenges 136
 Late Arrivals 136
 Reluctant Participants 136
 Constant Commentators 136
 Private Conversations 137
 Co-opters 137
 Put-Downs 137

Chapter 16—Telephone Manners 139
Answering the Telephone 139
Making Calls 141
Returning Calls 141
Voice Mail and Message Services 142
Home-Based Businesses 143
Using Cellular Telephones and Pagers 143
Avoiding Pitfalls 144
Telephone Interviews 145

Chapter 17—Conversational Manners 147
Showing Courtesy 147
 Discussing Controversial Subjects 148
 Interrupting 148
 Talking Too Much 148
 Talking above or down to Someone 148
 Telling Stories Repeatedly 149

Managing Your Image Potential

    Being a Good Listener 149
    Practising Plain Courtesy 149
    Admitting You're Wrong and Apologizing 150
Handling Compliments 150
    Acknowledging a Compliment 150
    Paying a Compliment 151
    Passing on a Compliment 151
Avoiding Pitfalls 151
    Personal Questions 151
    Unanswered Questions .152
    Bragging and Name Dropping 152
    Using Too Many Superlatives 153
    Obscene Jokes and Swearing 153
    Gossip 153
    Giving Unsolicited Advice 153
    Embarrassing Situations 154

Chapter 18—Verbal Communication **155**
    Tempo 155
    Tone 156
    Inflection 156
    Tips for a Healthy Voice .157
    Grammar and Sentence Structure 158

Chapter 19—Pregnancy Etiquette and the Workplace . . .**159**
    Announcing Your Pregnancy 159
        When to Make It 159
        How to Make It 160
    Maintaining Your Professional Image 161
    Managing Inappropriate Behaviour 162
    Handling Paternity Leave and Adoptions 163
    Choosing Professional Maternity Clothing 164

Chapter 20—Body Language 167

Chapter 21—Removing Communication Barriers from People with Disabilities 171
    Physical Impairment 172
    Hearing Impairment 173
        American Sign Language 174
        Preparing the Environment 174
        Preparing Yourself 175
        Acquired Hearing Loss in Seniors 176
    Visual Impairment 176
        Making Contact 176
        Crossing the Street 177
        Orienting the Person 177
        Using Language 177
        Approaching Doorways 177
        Approaching Stairs 178
        Sitting Down 178
        Additional Tips 178
    Additional Strategies for People with Disabilities 179

Chapter 22—Dining Protocol 181
    Please Take Your Seats 183
    Setting the Stage 184
        Flatware Is Placed Strategically 184
        From Outside to Inside 186
        Solids on the Left, Liquids on the Right 186
        Centre Stage 187
    Napkin Nuances 187
    Let the Dining Begin! 188
    Table Conduct 189
    Passing and Adding 191

Grasping the Glass 192
Implementing the Essentials .192
    Get a Grip on It! 193
    Cutting Remarks 194
Choosing Your Eating Styles .194
    American 195
    Continental 196
Positioning 197
    Pausing 197
    Finishing 198
Rolling along Smoothly 199
Soup's On! 200
Let Us Eat Salad 201
Dealing with Dinnertime Dilemmas 201
Dynamic Dessert Duo 204
Licence for Lip Balm and Lipstick 205
Special Dietary Needs 205
Dining Emergencies 206

Chapter 23—Business Mixers and Cocktails 209
Ten Tips on How to Work a Room 210
    1. Accept That Nervousness Is Natural 210
    2. Be Prepared 210
    3. Eat before You Go .210
    4. Dress Appropriately, but with Impact 211
    5. Make a Deliberate Entrance 211
    6. Never Approach a Group of Two 211
    7. Become the Host and Break the Ice 211
    8. Master Small Talk .212
    9. Focus on Contacts, Not Contracts 212
    10. Break Away Graciously and Continue to Network .212
Attending Private Cocktail Parties 213
Handling Liquid Refreshments 213

      Juggling Hors d'oeuvre and Canapés 214
      Devouring the Morsels 215

Chapter 24—Dining Conversation 217
      Turning the Conversation to Business 218
          During Breakfast 218
          During Lunch 218
          During Dinner 219

Chapter 25—Business Lunches and Dinners 221
      Hosting a Business Lunch .221
          Arranging the Lunch 221
          Before Your Guest Arrives 223
          During Lunch 223
          Handling the Bill 225
          After the Lunch 225
          Being a Polite Guest 226
          Being Interviewed at Meals 226
      Lunching with Colleagues .227
      Other Business-Related Meals 228
          Going-Away and Birthday Lunches 228
          Dinner Parties 228

Chapter 26—Hosting Large Business Functions 231
      Before the Event 232
      During the Event 233

Works Cited 235

Preface

Managing Your Image Potential: Creating Good Impressions in Business continues to be a work in progress. So many factors, trends and issues affect our personal and professional image that this book may very well be in a perpetual state of evolution. The pace of life and its constant dance of change greatly affect image management, so this book must be free to change as well.

As promised in the first edition, this second edition features helpful illustrations, new topics and improved treatment of many subjects. The perfect-bound presentation will also stand the test of time as you go back to chapters again and again.

In keeping with a spirit of openness and continual improvement, I welcome your suggestions for topics that need to be included or further elaborated on.

Acknowledgements

The keen interest shown in the first edition of *Managing Your Image Potential: Creating Good Impressions in Business* gave me the energy, excitement and motivation to develop this second edition, but it wasn't possible without the assistance of many others.

I'm indebted to my clients, students and image professionals around the world for their constructive criticisms and insights.

My thanks go to Kiara Emery, who went to the first edition of this book to research pregnancy etiquette in the workplace, and when she didn't find anything, suggested that I include the topic next time. I also want to thank the other mothers I interviewed for their stories and suggestions: Johanne Delves, Dianne Parke-Jones, Katherine Rudder, Natasha Taylor and Cathy Trant.

Thanks to Alana Cockburn of the Canadian Hearing Society for checking my information on communicating with people who are hard of hearing or deaf.

Graphic artist Diane Black of blackmac design has been a joy to work with. Her creative enthusiasm is evident in her excellent illustrations, layout and cover design.

My editor, Stephanie Stone, has been supportive of my writing, yet so merciless where it counts. Thank you for your vigilance in editing, your conceptualization and your great patience.

Like my first book, this edition has been a collaborative effort with my husband, Gregory, whose proofreading, research and ingenuity have been invaluable. Without his support and inspiration, I couldn't have accomplished this task.

About This Book

Shortly after I began working as an image professional, I found very few personal image management references for my clients and students. There are books covering the clothing aspect of image, but they're usually gender-specific. There are many excellent etiquette references, but some are so detailed that they become unwieldy for daily use. In *Managing Your Image Potential: Creating Good Impressions in Business*, I've attempted to collect information from a variety of sources into a concise guide for busy people. My focus is to provide practical knowledge that you can use to attain your image management goals.

I begin my book with an introduction to image management. You may not consider image important, but after considerable research, I was astounded to learn that in our visual society, it's pivotal to one's personal and professional success. Without image management, you seldom have the chance to show your real potential in today's competitive marketplace. In the first chapter, I've also added several examples to help you set your own image goals.

Chapter 2 puts clothing into its historical context and describes its social function and cultural expression. Several chapters then discuss how to use wardrobe strategies to give you a competitive edge.

Dressing in a business context has gone beyond the formula dressing of the 1980s to contextual dressing that fits the situation of the moment. However, there is tremendous confusion in the workplace about business casual dress. In Chapter 4, I've included some of the latest research into business casual trends, along with the key elements of three distinctive levels of business casual attire; this information will help you dress down without bottoming out.

In this revised edition, I've divided the original "Image Indicators" chapter into three chapters: "Establishing a Quality Image," "Men's Image Spoilers" and "Women's Image Spoilers." I've included a garment checklist as well as guidelines on quality fit and fabric selection. Separating the gender-specific issues allows you to quickly find the information you need. The men's chapter includes illustrations of the four basic tie knots, and in the women's chapter, the controversy over pants versus skirts continues.

The chapter on wardrobe planning is a basic overview of a process that takes time and experience to develop. With the help of the new basic wardrobe lists and module diagrams, you'll be saving time, energy and money as you develop a wardrobe that works for you. To help you select and care for your clothes, I've drawn on my expertise in textile technology to create a quick reference in Chapter 10.

The next sixteen chapters, which make up more than half the book, address the second aspect of image management—manners, etiquette and protocol. Although many of the topics apply in a social context, my focus is on proper behaviour in a professional setting. Before you become submerged in restrictions and rules, remember that caring for and being considerate of the person you're with is always your first priority.

Making an entrance, introducing people, holding up your end of a conversation, handling cellular phones and navigating the dining hour—the way in which you conduct yourself in all these aspects of your professional activities, and more, will be scrutinized and subsequently judged. Knowledge is a powerful social leveller; when you know how to act in a variety of situations, you'll be able to relax and attend to the business at hand.

In Chapter 12, I've added descriptions of handshakes to avoid in a business setting. In the chapter on improving your business image, one of the "Three Rs" of business has been changed to *respect*, which is often lacking when downsizing forces us to do more with less. Chapter 21 is a necessary reference to help you communicate effectively when you meet people with disabilities. Use the exercises in Chapter 18 to eliminate possible upward inflections in your voice, which rob you of credibility.

New to this edition are chapters on meeting manners, pregnancy in the workplace and hosting major business functions. I've also added extensive information on working a room and hosting a business lunch.

The purpose of *Managing Your Image Potential: Creating Good Impressions in Business* is quite clear: To impart knowledge and experience about image management that will serve you well. When we look at someone held in great esteem, we think that they have something that we don't. We're trained to think that only a tiny percentage of us can do great things. I believe that we all have the potential to excel in business and in life. Imagine your potential, and then use the image strategies in this book to achieve your career goals.

Catherine Graham Bell
August 2001

Chapter 1

Image Management Basics

Creating First Impressions

It takes less than ten seconds to create a first impression. In this time, the person you're meeting forms an opinion of your economic status, educational background, credibility and confidence. Your appearance, your voice, the words you use—even the car you drive—will influence their opinion of you.

When you were young, you were often admonished not to "judge a book by its cover," but one small detail of your appearance, or the tone of your voice, will far outweigh the words that you speak. There is an undeniable, primal reflex that is constantly at work in human beings. We instinctually and initially judge by appearances, either consciously or subconsciously. This fact about our human makeup is alarming. If you make a negative impression in those crucial few seconds, it's almost impossible to change it.

When you look for employment, a good education, and even appropriate experience, are no longer enough. In an interview, you need to "score high" immediately. If you don't, the interviewer is likely to ask you fewer questions, and listen to your answers with less interest, compared with another candidate who creates a favourable impression. Even if you have better education and more experience than others being interviewed, you may still not be successful in getting the job. There may be something in the interviewer's subconscious that influences the decision against you.

Research carried out in both the United States and the United Kingdom in the early 1990s showed that over 93 per cent of top decision makers involved in the hiring process agreed that personal presentation was the *key factor* in getting a job and advancing your career (Spillane 1993, 13). The more senior the manager being interviewed, the greater the importance they placed on the role of image in career success.

In today's competitive job market, if you're well groomed, appropriately dressed and have the right attitude, social graces and personality, you stand a good chance of being hired, even if your experience lacks some of the "hard skills" necessary for the position. It's much easier to acquire these skills than the "soft skills" associated with personal presentation.

Another study examined the sales process. It monitored salespeople from a broad range of fields—from computers to real estate—on their first-time sales calls with prospects.

> The conclusion: over half the time, the prospective clients decided within the first two minutes whether this was the kind of salesperson they wanted to work with...It was an emotional, visceral reaction. And for precisely that reason, it was a powerful one.
>
> The fact is that those first two minutes are critical in shaping prospects' perceptions of you, and particularly the extent to which they can trust your knowledge, integrity and professionalism. As a result, one of our key goals has to be to work as hard as possible on creating a positive initial impression in the first two minutes. (Richards 1999, 9)

Communicating Visually

The visual messages conveyed by your appearance are your most powerful form of communication. Experiments done by Dr. Albert Mehrabian (1981,76), a psychologist at the University of California at Los Angeles (UCLA), showed that our facial expression makes a greater impact on forming other people's opinion of us than our tone of voice or words.

The results were as follows:

Total liking = 7% verbal liking + 38% vocal liking + 55% facial liking

If you say all the right things in a job interview, but your behaviour contradicts your appearance or voice quality, you may not be successful. If you say that you're very interested in the position, but your facial expressions are bland and your posture suggests an uncaring attitude, the interviewers will probably doubt you. If you say that you pay attention to small details, but your shoes are unpolished and your grammar is questionable, they may not believe you.

Your visual image speaks volumes. For example, let's say a person dressed in torn blue jeans enters a high-quality clothing store for the first time. The salespeople would either ignore the person completely or follow them around the store, concerned that their merchandise may leave the establishment without passing by the cash register. Now suppose that the following month, the same person visits the store again, this time dressed in their finest suit. The attitude of the sales staff would now be friendly and helpful. You can see that the message communicated by the shopper's appearance has a definite impact.

In some extreme cases, the staff have actually told the shopper that he or she couldn't afford anything in the store; meanwhile, the shopper was affluent enough to purchase the entire establishment. Thus, your image *does* play a role in communication. The way in which you use your image will determine how well you'll be received by others and will ultimately affect your personal and professional success.

Setting Image Management Goals

Planning your career and personal life should include setting image management goals. Your image is just as important as deciding which career path to follow. If you spend years in post-secondary education and neglect the social and visual aspects of your image, you may not be given the opportunity to demonstrate your mastery of these professional skills. Undefined personal standards can lead to ignorant mistakes.

If your appearance or attitudes reflect another era, other people will question your awareness of current affairs. It's important to recognize current trends in clothing, hairstyles and glasses. So plan to update them at regular intervals. But never become a slave to fashion and blindly adopt an appearance that goes beyond your comfort zone. If you're not comfortable with your appearance, you won't be natural or self-empowered.

SMART Goals

Your goals should always be SMART:

Specific, **M**easurable, **A**ction-Oriented, **R**ealistic and **T**imely

Specific

If your goals aren't specific, setting goals becomes wishful thinking without direction. What do you want to achieve? How will you know whether you've achieved your goal? For example, a goal such as "I want to have a great job" is too vague. "I want to polish my image so that I'll be promoted to Human Resources Manager in six years" is much more specific. This large goal can be broken down even further.

Measurable

If your goal isn't measurable, how will you know if you've achieved it? While the above goal is specific, it's also ambitious. You can break it down into sub-goals that are measurable. For example: "I'll complete four Image Management courses with a B average in the next three years."

Action-Oriented

What actions do you need to take to achieve your goal? Develop a comprehensive, step-by-step plan of action. For example:

1. Register for a Business Protocol course.
2. Do all the necessary assignments and tests in a timely manner.
3. Pass the course.
4. Put into practice what I learned about business protocol.
5. Register for a course in Business Casual Dressing.

And so on.

Realistic

Is it possible for you to achieve this goal in the time frame you've established, given your present circumstances, abilities and other variables? For example, you may be overextended in other areas of your life and unable to commit the necessary time to reach your goal. It's possible to miss a step in your planning by forgetting an important element necessary to achieve your goal. By breaking down large goals into smaller steps, a huge task becomes more manageable.

Timely

Do your goals apply to where you are now, or do they reflect where you want to be in one, five or ten years? Set goals with appropriate timelines based on your personal and professional situation. Set short-term goals for one year, medium-term goals for two to five years, and long-term goals for anything beyond five years.

Using Positive Thinking

It's important to state your goals in a personal, positive, present-tense form. For example: "This week, I'm going to learn how to use my knife and fork properly by taking a dining protocol workshop on Tuesday evening. Then I'll feel comfortable at the head table at my best friend's wedding next month."

Your subconscious is a very powerful force in setting goals. For two decades, the Princeton Engineering Anomalies Research (PEAR) Laboratory has been studying the mind's power over random events (*DesignNews*, Spring 1997). It's discovered that a correlation exists between the mind and its ability to create tangible results.

If your goal is unattainable, or if it's too large to achieve in the time frame you've allocated, your subconscious will know this and will undermine your efforts. On the other hand, if your goal is SMART, you stand a greater chance of achieving it. Break a large, general image management goal, such as "I want to update my image," into several smaller, manageable goals.

Monitor and review your goals systematically. Once you've achieved them, set more goals. If your path has changed dramatically, re-evaluate where you are and adjust your goals accordingly.

Image Management Basics: Using Positive Thinking

As you complete each smaller, attainable step in your image management strategic plan, you'll be inspired to continue setting goals.

Maximize your potential:
Set SMART image management goals!

Chapter 2

Clothing in History

Throughout history, clothing, along with food and shelter, has been recognized as a primary need for all peoples in all parts of the world. Wearing clothing is common to both genders, regardless of age and socio-economic status.

Clothing provides protection against elements such as cold and heat and against insects and other physical hazards. Clothing provides varying degrees of modesty, depending on the climate and the individual customs of each culture. It's an integral aspect of the organization of societies, affecting group dynamics and economics.

Clothing made from beautiful fabrics in wonderful colour combinations not only fulfills an aesthetic need but also plays a part in growing economies. The economic growth of underdeveloped countries often parallels their investment in the manufacture of textiles and apparel goods.

As a Cultural Expression

Dress provides a great deal of information about the society in which it's evolved. It expresses the cultural patterns of the times and follows a path, or fashion cycle. This cycle moves from a time of inception, when a few innovators sport the look, through periods of general acceptance and eventually to the last stages of decline and obsolescence.

In certain periods of Western history, the fashions of the day reflected the prevalent social and political atmosphere. For example, during the French Revolution and the Napoleonic Wars, there were energetic fluctuations in design forms, whereas during the more stable era of Queen Victoria and the growth in industrial development, fashions were quite steady.

As a Social Function

Clothing provides primary links among people. It affects you, the wearer, and your audience. It conveys messages to every person you encounter. These messages cause others to form ideas about you and develop certain expectations that can influence the course of your relationship with them. As much as you may want to ignore the fact, your appearance has a greater effect on people you meet for the first time than any other factor (Mehrabian 1981, 76).

Clothing fulfills a psychological and emotional function. You may dress to fit in with peers and family, thereby satisfying a need for love and belonging. This is seen with children and adolescents in North America, who'll often refuse to wear anything but the latest trendy labels.

You can also raise your self-esteem by using clothing to increase your self-confidence. There is a freedom that comes from knowing you look your best, and this in turn instills an authentic sense of well-being. Of course, knowing that you're impressing someone also makes you feel good about yourself.

Clothing also has an interdependent relationship with social institutions associated with religious, political and economic structures. It helps organize society because it defines people's roles and status at different levels in the community. It can even be a powerful social force, especially in unstable societies, where the existing order is constantly changing. Uniformed police will often hold far greater status in countries where there is political unrest than in those where order has been established for some time.

Clothing is a powerful, non-verbal language. It can communicate to others an impression of social status, occupation, role, self-confidence, intelligence, conformity, individuality and other personality traits.

Maximize your potential:
Use clothing to your advantage!

Chapter 3

Wardrobe Strategies: Personal Criteria

We all approach clothing and appearance from our own perspective. The factors that affect your wardrobe choices are influenced by your personality, lifestyle and work environment. They may also be limited by personal beliefs, disabilities and allergies.

Recognizing Clothing Personalities

The sweater or tie that a well-meaning relative gives you for your birthday is sometimes relegated to the back of your closet. The garment fits, and it's in a favourite colour, but for some reason, you don't like it. When you put it on, you feel uncomfortable and immediately take it off; if you do wear it, it's out of obligation, and you can't wait to change into something else at the end of the day. This garment takes you out of the realm of your personal style. It's simply not "you."

Another example involves a woman who is a manager in the financial-services industry. A friend gave her a navy blue floral dress with a beautiful lace collar. She told me that although she'd received many compliments from her co-workers, she didn't feel comfortable wearing the garment. She was quite puzzled by this.

I then described to her the structured suits she usually wore, and I identified them as generally classic in style. In contrast, the floral dress was very romantic. Most people enjoy wearing one style of clothing more than another, and perhaps she preferred a classic style. Of course, her discomfort could also be connected to the context; wearing a feminine dress in a professional context didn't give her the look of authority that she needed as a manager.

Understanding your personality and how it relates to your wardrobe will help guide your clothing purchases. There are several different personalities:

- Classic
- Dramatic
- Romantic
- Natural

You'll usually find that you have one dominant personality and that you also relate to one or more of the other styles. In a working context such as that of the manager above, you may need to wear tailored classic clothing, which carries with it a sense of power. The feminine dress, which is romantic, may work for a more relaxed social function such as a garden party or wedding.

Classic

The classic personality is drawn to traditional clothing styles that are simple, understated and conservative. People who are classic feel quite happy in a structured garment such as a man's formal, three-piece, navy blue pinstripe suit or a woman's navy serge skirted suit.

The lines and textures of classic clothing aren't extreme. Plain fabrics, small or medium prints in traditional paisley patterns and polka dots, subtle checks, stripes and plaids in muted colour combinations can be found in accessory pieces such as ties and blouses.

Everything is in moderation. A classic person can safely invest in high-quality pieces because classic garments are usually timeless.

Dramatic

The dramatic personality is the opposite of the classic. Instead of timeless, conservative styles, the man or woman who is dramatic enjoys wearing garments that are striking, theatrical and creative. In a business context, dramatic people will wear the latest fashion trend, often with a structured, bold cut and a defined shoulder. Fabrics such as gabardines and smooth worsted wools will be stiffer, and prints and patterns will be in sharp, contrasting colours.

Accessories, which are never inconspicuous, continue the bold theme. Ties will make a strong statement, or they'll be monochromatic. Jewellery may have the appearance of fine sculpture, or it may be glamourous and glitzy. Dramatic people are never overlooked in a crowd.

Romantic

Someone who is romantic enjoys rich, luxurious clothing without the extremes of the dramatic person. Compared to the dramatic or classic styles, fabric choices will be soft, fine and draping. Soft, lightweight wools, challis, silk and buttery leather are favourites. Romantic women enjoy delicate florals, Victorian lace, ruffles and feminine colours. Romantic men are fashion-conscious, and their clothing has smooth, softly curved lines in rich, sometimes shimmering, fabrics. Accessories continue the soft story with solid silk ties and simple, elegant jewellery. Everything is tasteful, soft and subtle.

Natural

The typical natural person enjoys a casual look—sporty, outdoorsy and informal. If it's absolutely necessary to wear a jacket, the design will always be more sporty than the other personalities.

The cut of the clothing, especially in menswear, will be fuller, giving a roomy, comfortable fit. Natural men will prefer sports jackets to structured suits.

Natural women will prefer slacks to skirts. Garments will be in textured or rustic fabrics such as corduroy, flannel and tweed, with colour combinations that are in harmony with the outdoors. Nothing is shiny, fancy or too formal. For those who are natural, less is better than more.

Lifestyle Influences

Before you make a wardrobe plan, which will be discussed in the chapter on planning your wardrobe, it's important to also look at your lifestyle and how you spend your time. What type of work do you do? Are you a student? A homemaker? A working parent? A working single? A volunteer?

Do you work outdoors? In an office? At home? What kind of clothing do you wear for each activity? If you're a homemaker looking after very young children, you'll need functional pieces that can take you from home to a baseball game and then to a school meeting. You may be involved in planning charity events, which will require garments suitable for a gala evening, or casual clothes for an outdoor social occasion.

How do you spend your leisure time? Relaxing at home? Reading? Gardening? Sewing? Cooking? Shopping? Surfing the Internet? Playing sports? Visiting friends? Do these activities require clothing that is different from your work clothes? How much time do you spend doing each activity?

When do you need to dress up? Dining out or club hopping? Cultural events? Entertaining? Worship? Travel? Do you have clothing that is suitable for these occasions?

Once you've identified your various lifestyle needs, estimate the percentage of time you spend in each of these areas: work, casual and dressed up. Then analyze your closet to see whether the types of garments hanging there are roughly in the same percentages. If they're not, you may not be spending your wardrobe dollars in the areas of greatest need. If you own ten beautiful evening dresses, all purchased on sale, or three tuxedos, and you never have an occasion to wear them, this is false economy.

Whenever you make a major lifestyle change, your wardrobe needs usually shift. For example, let's say that for the past several years, you've been a student wearing blue jeans and sweatshirts. Now you're about to graduate and look for employment in the business world. If your closet doesn't contain any structured clothing, an "interview suit" will be a priority purchase. With careful planning and selection, this suit will become the basis of your new working wardrobe.

Another situation may arise if you're working for a while in a business environment wearing formal attire, then decide to take time out to raise a family, go back to school or simply retire. You'll realize that you own too many work clothes and need to buy new relevant pieces.

If you expect to re-enter the workforce in one to five years, you may want to carefully clean and store your classically styled, tailored clothing. As long as there have been no drastic changes in guidelines about how they should fit, classic garments will usually stand the test of time.

There is nothing that will date you more than a suit with a silhouette from another era. Often, a person leaves a profession in which they've worn a uniform for years, then attempts to resurrect a 20- year-old suit that is hardly worn and wear it to an interview or a social function. Although the suit may fit, subtle changes that have occurred over those 20 years will be evident. Consult a good tailor, who will determine whether a garment such as this can be altered to give you a more current look.

Work Environment

The second factor that influences your wardrobe is your work environment. Warehouse personnel would look out of place wearing tailored suits on the job. For someone working behind the counter at a fast-food chain, it wouldn't be appropriate to work in tattered jeans and a T-shirt. A restaurant chef draped in a fashionable creation won't function properly in the kitchen.

Dress is also affected by geographical location and customs. A bank manager working in a large city would usually wear a suit. If he or she worked in a small town surrounded by farms or logging camps, a more casual sports jacket would probably be an acceptable level of dress. If the environment is extremely relaxed, a shirt and tie, or a blouse worn with pants or a skirt, may be appropriate.

When you first start working for an organization and are unsure of the dress code, take your lead from your supervisor. If you dress one level higher than the position you're in, you'll be taken more seriously. When an opportunity for a promotion arises, you'll be considered before others who have to be groomed for the new position.

With the increase in entrepreneurship and small business, it's important to comment on the impact that your appearance can have on a new business. As mentioned in the first chapter on image management basics, first impressions are made in a few seconds;

people will decide whether to do business with you in just two minutes (Richards 1999, 9). If you become an entrepreneur, your wardrobe and appearance should be part of your strategic plan. You can spend a lot of time and money designing your logo, business cards, stationery, signage and promotion but forget your own image.

You are your business. What a potential client sees when they meet you will definitely affect the bottom line. Allocate a section of your business plan to strategically planning your personal image; then locate image professionals to help you communicate the message of professionalism and confidence you want.

Limiting Criteria

Besides clothing personality, lifestyle and work environment, there can be other limiting factors that affect your wardrobe strategies. For example, certain religious groups may require adherents to wear specific articles of clothing that differ from Western, secular norms.

Physical Disabilities

Physical disabilities will also narrow your choices. For example, you may have a disability that requires you to sit in a wheelchair for most of the day. Comfort and safety will be your primary needs. Wearing knitted or soft woven fabrics, with construction techniques that place flat seams toward the front of the garment, can help avoid skin complications.

If you're a businesswoman in a sector where a skirted suit is the norm and you wear special orthopaedic footwear to walk comfortably, you have a communication challenge. Your heavy shoes will call attention to your feet. Wearing a matched, tailored pantsuit in a dark, solid colour will ensure a powerful, professional effect. This strategy will help divert attention from your footwear to your face, giving you a better communication advantage. In some situations, it may be necessary to educate and persuade your employers that this less conventional approach to business attire is the best choice for you.

Allergies

Allergies to textile fibres can also affect your clothing choices. Although wool is nature's miracle fibre because it drapes and tailors superbly, you may have a sensitivity or an allergy to it. The better the quality of the wool fibre, the softer the fabric will be. Many people who say they have an allergy to wool may only have a sensitivity to it. They may have only worn the coarser qualities, fondly called *bull's wool*. Fabric made from this quality will usually irritate and scratch. Place the sleeve of the garment underneath your chin to check for *barbs*, which cause some wools to prickle and irritate the skin.

Before you write off wool completely, try a finer-quality cloth. The best-quality wool fibres are very small in diameter and have tiny barbs that you can't feel; fabrics made from these fibres will have a very soft, smooth *hand* (the way it feels). *Cool wool*, which was developed by the Australian wool industry through the International Wool Secretariat, not only has this smooth hand, but it's also so light that it's comfortable to wear in the warmer months.

If you do have a genuine allergy to wool, advancements in synthetic fibres make them a viable alternative. Polyester, nylon and rayon made in small microfibre diameters produce fabrics that drape beautifully. It's better to consider these more expensive fabrics than to purchase inexpensive versions that have poor quality and appearance.

The opposite problem also exists. You may not be able to wear synthetics and have to rely on natural fibres. Except for wool, which seldom wrinkles if handled properly, natural fibres crease easily, so they require more care. When you choose wool, you must also remember to include the cost of dry cleaning in your wardrobe budget.

Maximize your potential:
Apply your own wardrobe criteria!

Chapter 4

Your Competitive Edge: Wardrobe Communication

Dressing for Your Company Culture

Every business has a dress code. Some companies may have strict, written guidelines that are communicated to each new employee and diligently enforced. Others may say that they have no dress code, but when the principals are questioned further, they admit that they do have certain expectations regarding the appearance of their employees. This is an implied dress code.

As a potential employee, you need to determine what a company's clothing guidelines are to ensure that you're in sync with its culture. If you're visiting a business for the first time, err on the side of formality. It's always safer to appear overdressed than too casual. If you're going for a job interview, call the reception desk and ask for general information regarding the company's dress code. Another way to do research is to visit the company location beforehand and watch people entering and leaving.

Once you get a job, you'll want to dress to fit into the company culture. Take note of the clothing being worn by your peers and your supervisor. It's prudent to dress at least as well as your peers, and if you want to be noticed, slightly better. If you dress for the position that is one level higher than yours, you're communicating that you have your eye on advancement. You're projecting your potential for success, and assuming that you possess the necessary skills, you'll often be considered for promotion ahead of others.

You may be faced with a situation where your supervisor doesn't dress appropriately for his or her position. If you took your lead from this person, you'd be doing yourself and the company a disservice. Don't be concerned about dressing better than your supervisor. If you sense that this is threatening to them, use a positive, supportive attitude to dispel their fears.

Dressing for the Context

In the early 1980s, many companies recognized the value of a polished appearance and organized Dress for Success seminars for their employees. In those years, the successful look for a man consisted of a navy blue suit, a white or subtle, pinstriped shirt, and a classically patterned, burgundy tie. Women were relegated to wearing a navy blue skirted suit, a white or pastel blouse and either a scarf tied at the neck or a string of pearls. Dressing in this manner was understood by all, it was very safe.

In the 1990s, companies began experimenting with dressing down, and the dress-for-success look was no longer the norm. Specifically, companies involved in computer technology switched to an everyday casual dress code. Financial institutions followed more cautiously with "casual Fridays." To justify this change in dress code, employees were asked to contribute a small sum of money to a charity for the privilege of dressing down for the day.

However, relaxing dress codes raised several concerns. Many employees didn't understand what was appropriate for *business casual* dress. They arrived for work in tattered jeans, T-shirts emblazoned with lewd slogans or their favourite beer, tank tops, short shorts and bra tops. In response, some companies either rushed to put acceptable casual-dress guidelines into writing; others banned dressing down entirely and reverted to the formal business attire that was unequivocally understood. Some businesses now insist that employees who deal with the public dress formally, while those who have no contact with the public can wear anything.

On the other hand, there is the case of the call centre that has begun to enforce a strict, formal dress code for all employees, even for those who spend their whole day speaking to customers on the telephone. Management believes that employees who dress professionally will have greater self-esteem; this positive attitude will be transmitted to their customers over the telephone. Management realizes that appearance is an essential strategy that it can use to attract and keep customers in a competitive marketplace.

It's not surprising that casual attire has created a lot of confusion in the workplace. An article that appeared in *USA TODAY* in June 2000 stated that while most companies usually research strategic decisions thoroughly, the trend to dressing down has gone through the industry with little research at all. The article also outlined some statistics associated with casual dressing.

> Concerned that laissez-faire policies on casual dress undermine professionalism, many employers are asking workers to dress up instead of down. They're cracking down on a trend that some believe has hurt the corporate image, encouraged slacking off and fostered environments ripe for sexual harassment.
>
> The number of companies permitting casual attire has declined for the first time since 1992, although a lopsided

> majority still allows casual dress, based on a Society for Human Resource Management poll. In 1998, 97% of companies allowed staffers to dress casually either every day or once a week. [In 2000], that number dropped to 87%.
>
> In a survey of 1,000 companies by Jackson Lewis, a law firm based in White Plains, N.Y., employers were asked whether they had noticed an increase in absenteeism and tardiness after instituting a casual dress policy. Nearly half said yes, and 30% reported a rise in flirtatious behavior. (Armour 2000)

In environments where strict dress guidelines have loosened up, you need to consider many factors when you dress each morning. If you're working in a sector where you'll be seeing clients from several social or business backgrounds, you'll need to learn to dress contextually. For example, if you're an insurance agent, you may have appointments with different types of people in one day: the CEO of a corporation, a local farmer and a young family investigating insurance for the first time. If so, you can use wardrobe strategies to your advantage.

If your credibility is an issue when you visit the corporation, wearing a navy suit with pants or a skirt, a shirt or blouse and (if you're a man) a tie will have a powerful effect. Just removing the jacket will be dressing down sufficiently for the farmer, who will expect some form of business attire but may be intimidated by the matching jacket. (If you must wear a jacket, a sports jackct in a subtle pattern will make you more approachable than the suited look.) If you think that the young couple may also be intimidated by business attire, you may want to remove the tie and put on a sweater.

Dressing down too far can be dangerous because it can make you lose your credibility. This is especially true for women. When men dress down, they lose some authority; when women dress down, they seem to lose *all* authority. To illustrate this point, a study carried out at the University of Manitoba (Temple and Loewen 1993, 345) showed that a woman wearing a jacket was perceived to have greater expertise and legitimate power than a woman not wearing a jacket. We may question this business cultural norm, but it does exist. If you choose not to use this wardrobe strategy to your advantage, be prepared to expend extra effort to project a professional image.

Dressing Down by Degrees

Each social or professional context may require you to wear different degrees of casual dress. There are five variables that affect the perceived formality or informality of your outfit.
- the number of pieces of clothing you're wearing
- the colour combinations
- the pattern and texture of the fabric
- the style of your garments
- the style and materials of your accessories

Clothing Pieces

The greater the number of pieces of clothing you wear at one time, the greater the degree of formality you exhibit. When you reduce the number of pieces of clothing, the outfit becomes more casual.

- At the most formal end of the scale, you'll find a three-piece suit with a jacket, vest, pants or skirt, worn with a shirt or blouse and a tie, if applicable.

- Pants worn with a T-shirt will be at the most casual end of the scale.

- In business, where dressing has become more casual, you seldom see a vest being worn under a jacket, unless it's worn under a sports coat and in a contrasting colour or texture.

Colour Combinations

Colour works on emotional, instinctual and cultural levels. In our Western society, dark colours project an image of power and authority.

- The darker the colour you wear, the more powerful an image you'll project, especially when dark shades are combined with high-contrasting colours. For example, a suit in black or navy has the greatest strength and formality when it's worn with a blouse or shirt in white or ecru.

- If you take the same dark suit and put with it a mid-tone shirt or blouse, such as French blue, you'll be dressing down one level.

- Switching from dark colours to mid-tones, such as a mid-grey or taupe, makes your appearance less formal. The reception you receive wearing a taupe suit will be remarkably different than if you wear a navy one.

- Combining a jacket of one colour with pants or a skirt of another colour will dress down the look as well. Such two-tone combinations will always be less formal than a matched suit.

- Classic tones of navy, black, taupe and grey are more formal than bright colours usually associated with casual attire.

- If you're a manager and want to meet with your staff to ask them for their opinions, take one of these less formal approaches.

Fabric Texture and Pattern

The smoother and plainer the fabric, the more formal a garment will be. Once you start adding texture and/or pattern to your garments, you achieve a more casual effect.

- A plain-coloured, smooth worsted wool or a polyester microfibre will always have a polished appearance.

- A tweed jacket in a plaid pattern is a good example of a more casual approach.

- If you need a formal or powerful look, keep floral and paisley prints to a minimum in ties, shirts, blouses, skirts and dresses. A floral tie or a paisley blouse will soften a navy suit, but if the prints are worn from head to toe, the resulting effect takes you closer to the casual end of the scale.

- When you replace woven fabrics with knitted fabrics, the effect becomes even more casual. If, for example, you're wearing a jacket with a woven dress shirt and you want to soften your look, replace the shirt with a knitted polo shirt or turtleneck. (Make sure that the knitted fabric is compact and lightweight because heavier versions are usually associated with weekend wear.)

- The quality of the fabric also affects your impact. Worsted wools and silks are considered better quality and therefore more formal than cottons, linens and synthetic blends. Good-quality microfibres, as mentioned before, can be a substitute for wool if you have allergies.

- A pair of worsted wool pants is far more formal than denim jeans. If you wear jeans in a business context, you may need to wear a blazer to lift them from the bottom of the formality scale.

Garment Style

The style of your garments also affects how your outfit is perceived.

- A matched suit is more powerful than a blazer worn with pants or a skirt.
- A tailored, collared shirt is more formal than a collarless shirt, blouse or T-shirt. This is especially true for men.
- A fully tailored garment carries more weight than a soft, unconstructed version.
- Unless you reside in Bermuda or the tropics, shorts are never proper business attire.
- If you're a woman, take note: Wearing a dress has less impact than wearing a suit, unless the dress is a structured coat dress in a dark colour or you wear the dress with a jacket.
- In some companies, women wearing skirts are seen as more professional than those who wear slacks.
- If you're negotiating a large contract, a skirt and blouse alone won't give you the credibility you'll need; a jacket is essential.
- Garments that are too revealing can compromise your position and your power.
- You don't wear dressy or formal garments for business, just as a business suit is out of place at an informal social gathering.

Accessories

The style of your accessories, and the materials they're made of, are determined by the context.

- Wear fine accessories with tailored, professional attire—for example, shoes with thin soles, fine jewellery in gold or silver, high-quality leather portfolio and/or purses, etc.

- With business casual clothing, your accessories can be bolder and heavier. Consider shoes with thicker soles, chunky jewellery in materials such as bone or pewter, canvas attaché cases and/or purses, etc.

Three Levels of Business Casual

In addition to the five factors that indicate the degree of formality, there are three levels of business casual dressing. Your approach will depend on your work environment.

Tailored Business Casual

The key element at this level is a *tailored jacket*. It's usually worn with a contrasting pair of pants or skirt for a two-tone look. A shirt, blouse, polo shirt, mock turtleneck or full turtleneck can be worn underneath. This look is chosen by people who normally wear a suit to work and don't want to be too casually dressed at any time.

Smart Business Casual

The key element of smart business casual for men is a *collared shirt* (including mock turtlenecks and full turtlenecks). For women, a collared shirt is not essential but preferred. Even within this category, there is quite a range of formality. A combination of dress shirt, trousers and tie are at the top end, with a polo shirt and cotton pants near the bottom. Most companies researched favour smart business casual on dress-down Fridays.

Relaxed Business Casual

Instead of one key item, there are a number of fabrics and styles that are associated with this level: denim (both blue and other colours), T-shirts, sleeveless garments, shorts, fleece, running shoes and casual sandals. If there are any slogans on the clothing, companies prefer that it be their firm's logo, not that of your favourite beverage. This level of dress has been adopted by people working mainly in the information technology sector.

Your wardrobe should contain a variety of business suits, business casual looks and weekend casual garments. Learn to strategically plan your wardrobe for every possible business occasion—your clothing will speak volumes about you and your future.

Maximize your potential:

Gain a competitive edge using strategic wardrobe communication!

Chapter 5

Using Clothing Details to Your Advantage

You can work the elements and principles of design used to create clothing to your advantage. You can use them to either draw the viewer's eye quickly to your face or to distract and delay the eye contact that is so vital to good communication. The combination of the outline of your body and the lines of your clothing can greatly affect your overall proportions and the point to which the eye is drawn. You can create optical illusions with your clothing to emphasize your good features and draw the eye away from possible figure challenges.

Clothing should be in proportion to your body features, height, weight and bone structure. You can use fabric texture, pattern and colour to successfully balance your body shape. Jacket length, and for women, skirt, jewellery and dress lengths, should be in keeping with your vertical proportion. What is appropriate for you may not suit someone else. You must develop an informed sense of personal style, striving for balance in all things, including your appearance.

Analyzing Your Body Features

We all have unique body features. Accepting them can be a powerful tool for attaining personal fulfillment and success. The "ideal body type" is always fluctuating, subject to the whims of popular culture. The truth is that the ideal body type is often unattainable. In fact, the definition of *ideal* in anything can be justifiably questioned. What is most important is to know your own body shape well and learn how to dress to accentuate your best features. If you think that you have a figure challenge that is a distraction, and if you want to, you can camouflage it by using the elements and principles of design.

The first step is to carefully analyze your body type. The techniques for men and women are the same. Stand at least two metres (six feet) from a full-length mirror and take a good look at yourself. Are your chest and hips well balanced, or is one area much larger than the other? Does your abdomen protrude, drawing attention to your waistline? Are your shoulders tapered or square? When you wear a crewneck T-shirt, does your neck tower above the neckband, suggesting that you have a long neck? If you wear a turtleneck, are you swallowed up by the collar, showing that your neck is short?

These are some questions to consider before you begin your wardrobe purchases. An image consultant or fashion designer can help you accurately assess your personal characteristics and give you direction on your best clothing and accessory styles. Today, many image consultants use computer-assisted diagnostic programs as tools in these assessments.

Lines Carry the Eye

The lines created both by the outer edge of your garment, and the design details within, will carry the viewer's eye from your feet to your face. If there are a lot of vertical lines and few horizontal ones to distract the eye, this journey will be quick. If you want to look taller, capitalize on keeping the eye moving up.

Vertical lines, which can be created by a row of vertical buttons or the outer edge of a slim pant, will make you look taller and thinner. Horizontal lines, seen where a black pant and a white shirt meet at the waist, or in horizontal stripes, will make you look shorter and wider. Diagonal lines will carry the eye up—the longer the diagonal line, the greater the lengthening and slimming effect will be. The line created by a jacket's lapel, if it's in contrast to the shirt, is a good example of this.

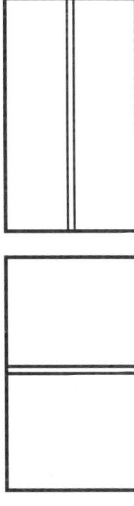

Curved lines will slow the eye down and add more roundness and fullness to your figure. Round lines are found in the curved hem of a jacket, in a large paisley or polka-dot print and along the edge of a scalloped lace collar.

Focusing on the Face

Collars frame your face, so select them carefully according to your face shape, neck length, shoulder width and shoulder slope. Use collars to direct the viewer to look at your eyes. Poor collar and neckline choices can become a distraction to communication and can emphasize extreme facial features.

For example, if you have a narrow, pointed chin, wearing a V-neck will emphasize this feature through *repetition*; a round neckline would be a better choice. If you have a round face, avoid adding to the fullness by wearing a round neckline. If your shoulders are narrow and sloped, take care to choose horizontal shoulder yokes, square necklines or boat necks, which go straight across you from shoulder to shoulder. An interesting tie or scarf can also bring the viewer's focus to your face.

I've seen many people with short necks wearing turtlenecks that come so high under their chin that the collar seems to swallow up their heads. Instead of listening to what they're saying, my eyes go to their collars, and I subconsciously fold them down two or three times. Make sure that the collar isn't wearing you, but that you're wearing the collar.

Communicating with Colour

Colour has the power to affect our emotions and the reactions of the people around us. Red will give you a boost and command the attention of your audience, while blue has a calming, soothing effect. Avoid wearing red if you want to be seen as a team player. Brown on men doesn't fare well in an interview situation, and avoid yellow if you want to be taken seriously. Monochromatic colour combinations can create a sophisticated image; a mixture of bright colours in a formal business setting will produce a jarring effect. You can use colour to make you more approachable or powerful, as described in the chapter on wardrobe communication. It can also produce a healthy glow or cause you to look sallow.

Colour can create balance by enlarging or decreasing an area of your body. Bright, warm colours such as yellow, orange, red and bright green, as well as white and tints, will make an area of your body larger because they appear to *advance*. Dark, muted, cool colours such as navy, forest green, burgundy, grey and black cause the area in which they're used to *recede* and appear smaller. This is called *colour blocking*; use it to your advantage. If your hips are much larger than your chest, use darker colours on your lower body and brighter colours on the upper area. Use small areas of bright colour in a tie or scarf to draw the viewer's eye to your face.

Don't underestimate the effect of colour on your skin tone. Most people fall into either a cool or warm skin-tone category. When you're wearing colours that are in harmony with your individual colouring, you'll look well rested, younger, healthy and vibrant. Facial lines and shadows will be smoothed out, and your eyes will sparkle.

When you wear colours that aren't in your colour palette, you'll appear tired and possibly jaundiced (yellow). Blemishes or skin irritations will become more obvious, dark circles may appear around your eyes and the colour will drain from your face.

If your skin is *cool*, you have predominantly blue undertones. You'll look good in colours that also have blue undertones, such as blue-reds, blue-greens and blue-pinks. Most olive-skinned people and those of African descent look best in cool tones, but some with lighter, golden skin may come alive in warm colours.

If you have ivory, peach or golden-beige skin tones, your skin is probably *warm*. You'll look good in colours that have yellow undertones, such as peach, orange-reds, golds, yellow-greens and beiges. Most redheads look best in colours from the warm palette, but occasionally, a redhead will look better in cool colours.

To discover your best colour palette, you can experiment by comparing pairs of cool and warm colours, but it's best to use the expertise of a colour consultant, who has a trained eye. Once you know your personal colours, coordinating your wardrobe will be much easier because you'll find that colours in your palette will usually blend well.

When many people "got their colours done" in the early 1980s, they'd often take their seasonal swatches to a clothing store to look for garments to match one of their swatches exactly. They usually left empty-handed. There are thousands of variations for each hue, and the likelihood of finding an exact match is slim. Use colour swatches you receive from an image consultant only as a *guide* to direct you towards a particular colour family.

Other people found that they didn't look their best in black or dark navy and began avoiding these powerful colours. However, these are corporate colours, and everyone needs them. If they're not your best colours, add a shirt and tie or blouse in coordinating colours from your palette. As long as the colour near your face is in keeping with your skin tone, you'll be successful in straying from your palette for your secondary pieces of clothing. Of course, you can wear makeup to alter your skin tone, but not everyone chooses to wear it.

If you colour-enhance your hair, be careful. Remember to consider your skin tone when selecting a dye colour. If you have cool skin tones and dye your hair a warm red, you'll experience the same negative effects as when you wear colours from the warm palette. That's because your new hair colour will be out of harmony with your natural skin tone. Again, changing your makeup can counteract this to some degree. However, when you're faced with the clothes in your closet, which you bought to harmonize with your natural colouring, it may be difficult to choose something that now looks good on you.

Texture Creates Illusions

You can use texture, like colour, to give the illusion of enlarging and decreasing your body shape. Fabrics that are bulky, stiff and thick will *increase* and are effective in areas you want to look larger. For example, if you have a large chest and don't want to increase it, create balance by using a bulky corduroy in pants or a skirt; keep the fabric you use in the chest area a lighter weight and less bulky.

Shiny fabrics reflect light and also increase size, so avoid using them in areas of your body that you want to appear smaller. If you're short, be careful not to wear shiny fabrics from head to toe because they'll overwhelm you. It's better to use them in accessories such as a blouse, scarf or tie to draw attention to your face; this will also make you appear taller. Fabrics that are lightweight, with good drape and a matte finish, make your whole body or an area of your body look smaller. These are also good choices for a short person because they won't overpower you.

Pattern Balances Proportions

The pattern of the fabric in your garments works best when it's in proportion to your height, weight and bone structure. Medium-sized prints and checks can be worn by everyone and will often camouflage a figure challenge more than a plain fabric.

Tall people, or those who are of medium height with a large bone structure, can wear medium-to-large prints. Those who are short and have a medium-to-small bone structure will look better in small-to-medium patterns.

Full-figured people are best in medium-sized prints. Small patterns will make you look larger because of the contrast between the size of the print and your body size; large prints will increase your figure as a result of repetition.

The colours used in prints can make you appear larger or smaller. A small person will be overpowered by a large pattern in bright colours. However, they may be able to wear the same pattern in tones that are all dark or all light because the size of the print isn't as noticeable.

Patterns, such as plaids and checks that are a combination of straight, geometric lines, will be more slimming than organic prints that primarily use curved lines. However, this enlarging effect will be lessened if the curved motifs are set into geometric boundaries or blocks.

Vertical stripes lengthen a body, while horizontal stripes are usually associated with creating width. Horizontal stripes won't always make you look shorter, however; if they're thin and spaced apart, they can act like a ladder and lead the eye up your body. Similarly, wide vertical stripes won't make you look thinner; when stripes become wide, the viewer's eye tends to go horizontally from stripe to stripe, giving the perception of a broader figure.

Maximize your potential:

Choose clothing details in harmony with your body shape!

Chapter 6

Establishing a Quality Image

After you've chosen your clothing, taken into consideration your body shape, the level of formality that is appropriate for your work environment and the message you want to communicate, there are several other points to consider that will help you polish your image.

Quality Counts

No one ever regrets buying quality. Whether you're talking about clothing, accessories, cars or computers, when you invest in a quality product, the item will last longer, perform better and require less maintenance. If you're enticed to buy an item of clothing based solely on price, remember the old adage "You get what you pay for" holds true when buying your attire too.

Although it costs more initially, purchasing a higher-quality item will always double or triple the life of your clothing and accessories. Consider the case of buying a leather portfolio. Let's say you're deciding between two items. The higher-priced item is made from excellent leather; the other one, which is half the price, looks almost the same, but the hide used in the construction was first split into two thinner pieces before it was dyed and finished.

During the first six months, both portfolios will wear about the same. It's after this time that the quality of the leather will determine the life of the items. The better-quality portfolio should last three to five times as long as the inexpensive one, and as it ages, it'll do so gracefully. If a quality appearance is essential, you'll need to replace the cheaper portfolio every one to two years.

Clothing Details

Whether you're considering keeping a garment in your closet or making a new purchase, be sure to examine its fabric, construction and fit and whether its style is close enough to current fashion trends.

Fads, Fashion Trends and Classics

Fads that go in and out of favour in a matter of months are poor investment pieces and not appropriate for business. Fashion trends take two or three years to run their cycle. Having something fashionable in your wardrobe shows that you're not out of touch with what's going on in the world; however, leave the trend behind when it's over, or you'll quickly look dated. If you enjoy high fashion but it's not usually worn at your place of work, tone it down or wear it in personal contexts. If you're working in the fashion or artistic fields, you'll be expected to be aware of trends and reflect them in your attire. Classics are always in style and often flattering to everyone; try to use them as the basis of your wardrobe.

Fabric Guidelines

The quality of the fabric used in a garment will affect not only the life of the piece but also the way it drapes and performs. Clothing that performs well doesn't need a lot of upkeep or pressing if you hang and store it properly. You should be able to take it out of your closet and put it on immediately.

• Air out your clothing at the end of the day before storing it in your closet. This not only allows moisture to evaporate, which prolongs the life of your clothing, but also lets creases fall out. This is especially true of garments made from wool.

• You'll find that cotton and linen will require more upkeep because of their natural tendency to crease. The creases that come with a shirt made from pure cotton, compared to one in a cotton-and-polyester blend, are readily overlooked by those who appreciate quality. Natural-fibre shirts that crease must be laundered after each wearing, so be prepared to wash them yourself or send them out to a laundry.

• The higher the quality of the fibre that goes into the fabric, the more likely the garment is to hang or drape well. Cheaper fibres will often be more bulky, crease more and have a rough appearance. Garments made from good-quality fibres will always feel better when you wear them. When you feel good in your clothes, it's easier for you to project confidence and poise. For more detail on fibres, see the chapter on fibre characteristics and care.

• Dyeing and finishing techniques will also affect the final product. Some time ago, I purchased an inexpensive silk blouse in a bright fuchsia colour. Even after 20 washings, the rinse water continues to turn dark pink. Although this garment seemed like a good purchase, the time I've spent taking care to wash it on its own has made me regret buying it.

- Inexpensive fabrics will sometimes *crock*. This means that the dye on the fabric will rub off on garments worn either under or over them. New denim jeans that haven't been pre-washed will always leave traces of indigo on undergarments. Most dark-coloured garments made in natural fibres will bleed the first time as excessive dyestuff is washed away. You should see little or no dye migration after the first washing, except for items made from denim, which are meant to fade each time.

- Fabrics made from tightly woven or knitted cloth will usually perform better than those made in looser constructions. Some inexpensive fabrics that are woven loosely often have starch or sizing applied to give them weight and body. The first laundering removes this finish, leaving behind a garment that is limp and that may also have shrunk.

Construction

Besides the fibre, fabric construction and finishing, the actual make-up of a garment will affect its quality. The more sewing and hand work that has gone into it, the higher the price will be.

For example, it takes an experienced tailor 36 hours to hand-tailor a man's suit jacket. The interfacing, interlining, lining and specialized stitching support the outer fabric and shape the garment. Beneath the exterior wool fabric, which can be surprisingly lightweight, are at least four layers of fabric. Three of the layers are expertly moulded to create a curved support that closely resembles your chest. The fourth layer is the inner lining, which camouflages the inner construction and helps the jacket glide on and off with ease.

A lined garment will last longer, hang better and be more comfortable to wear. As its price goes down, the amount of hand work is reduced. Most men's ready-made suits are now made with pre-assembled, layered interfacing panels.

The types of seams used and the number of stitches per centimetre are also aspects of quality. A better-quality garment will have enough seam allowance to allow for the seams to be let out. If seams that have been overcast with serging don't have enough thread, they won't be strong and will fray. Knitted garments require specialized seams to ensure that they'll stretch with you without breaking. Avoid any garment with puckered stitching; a good pressing can't make up for poor construction.

Buttons can make or break a garment. Consider changing inexpensive buttons on a basic garment to ones that have a look of quality. You'll immediately experience the power of small details to transform and renew.

Construction Checklist

When you buy clothing, although you expect the garment to be perfect, this is not always the case; it pays to look closely at the fabric and construction. Using this checklist, you can ensure that garments are well made, fit properly and are generally of high quality. This quality will contribute to the professional image you want to convey.

Garment Details	✔
Is the fabric in good condition? (Is there any sign of wear at the seat, knees, elbows or hems? Is there any pilling or surface wear? Are there any stains?)	
Does the garment hang well? (Does it pull at the seams or hems?)	

Is the garment lined? If so, is the lining in good condition? (A worn lining can usually be replaced, and if the rest of the garment is in good condition, this is worth the expense.)
Is the garment well supported? (Does it have good interfacing in the collar, cuffs, front, waistband, etc.?)
Is there enough seam allowance inside the garment to allow for alterations? Are the seam allowances finished, or are they raw and ravelling?
Are the seams flat, or are they puckering?
Are the buttons in good condition? Do they need to be changed?
Are the buttonholes in good condition, or do they show signs of fraying?
Is the zipper inserted correctly so that it lays flat?
Are the pockets in good repair? (Are there holes in the pocket lining? Are there tears at the stress points?)
Is the garment cut on the straight grain? (Does it hang straight, or does it twist to one side?)
If the fabric is patterned, does the pattern match at the seams?
Does the collar roll nicely, or does it crack or break along the roll line?
Do the hems lie flat, and are they even?
Are the seams at the edges pressed flat and rolled to the inside, or are they bulky and obvious?
Are the shoulder pads in good condition? (Do they pull? Are they matted and uneven?)
Are the belt loops intact and in good repair?

Fit

The fit of your clothing is a reflection of quality. You can pay a large sum for a quality garment, but if you haven't taken the time to make sure it fits properly, it'll have the appearance of an inexpensive piece. Many people who dislike shopping are notorious for rushing into a store, trying on a garment and leaving before they know it fits properly.

Ready-to-wear is made to fit a well-proportioned body shape. If you're between sizes, or if one area of your body is out of proportion to another, you'll need to spend the time, and often the money, to have a garment altered appropriately.

In most independent menswear stores, the price of alterations is included in the cost of the clothes. Most womenswear stores charge extra for alterations. I recommend having the alterations done at the store where you buy a garment. If it doesn't fit exactly right, or if an extra piece of fabric is necessary to make it fit, it's easier for you to deal with the retailer. The owner of the store also appreciates the opportunity to send you on your way looking impeccable. After all, their image is ultimately tied to yours.

Fit Guidelines

When you're considering a garment for fit, follow these guidelines:

- Avoid clothing that is too tight or too loose. When a garment is tight, the contours of the body, and sometimes the outline of undergarments, detract from quality details. When it's too loose, the garment looks sloppy. Buy a garment to fit the largest part of your body and, if necessary, have it altered to fit the rest of you. For example, if you have a well-developed upper body or a large bust, when you buy a jacket, choose a size that is large enough for these areas.

The hipline of the garment may need to be taken in as well.

• Impeccable fit of the collar and shoulders of a suit jacket or coat is essential. A good tailor can usually make alterations to this area so that it lies smoothly, without any wrinkles. If the collar stands away from the back of your neck or gapes at the sides, it needs shortening. If too much or too little of your shirt collar is showing, the jacket collar can be raised or lowered. These changes are usually easier to make with menswear because designers design with alterations in mind.

• If you have an obvious body feature such as an extreme head-forward posture, or if there is a large discrepancy between your upper and lower body, a garment may need to be made to measure. If you choose good-quality fabrics, this will be an investment piece that will serve you well. Sometimes you can order stock separates (a top of one size and a bottom in a different size).

• Your pants must be long enough. They should come slightly above where your heel meets your shoe in the back, with a crease in the front so that when you walk, they don't ride up too far.

• Jackets will be large investment pieces. If the jacket is the wrong length, it won't give you good, balanced proportion. The length of the jacket is influenced by the jacket style and the relationship of your body and legs to your overall height. Advice from a retailer, designer, tailor or image consultant will guide you in this matter.

• Sleeves shouldn't be too long or too short. Although sleeve length is a personal decision, jackets should usually come past your wristbone to the first joint on your thumb; shirt sleeves should come one-half inch (1.25 cm) more. Remember, fashion trends can change what is acceptable at any given time.

Exaggerated Patterns and Colours

Loud or flashy patterns and colours don't project an image of quality. Garments in these combinations will become dated quickly, and you'll tire of them more easily than classic colours and patterns. If you want the excitement of these colours and patterns, relegate them to low-investment pieces such as ties and scarves. Plain-coloured or subtly patterned garments will last longer and can be dressed up or down to fill a variety of business and social needs. Classic patterns include muted checks, stripes and plaids.

Gently Used Clothing

Second-hand stores can be a source of clothing that is of high quality and at a fraction of its original cost. Before purchasing a garment, examine it carefully using the fabric, construction and fit guidelines provided earlier in this chapter. Next, try the garment on and compare it to the general style of the day. (Apply this scrutiny to the clothing in your closet as well.) If you're not educated in these matters, acquire the services of an image or fashion consultant. Altering will update some garments, but not all.

There is nothing worse than seeing someone totally out of sync with the times, no matter how much life is left in the garment they're wearing. A garment long past its era isn't a bargain at any price. It's usually better to invest in a few pieces of current, quality clothing that you can coordinate with other garments in your closet. Don't sacrifice your credibility for the sake of a few dollars.

Accessories

Your accessories tell others a lot about you and your attention to detail. Strive to select quality accessories coordinated to the style and colour of your clothing. A leather briefcase, portfolio, purse or billfold will look better and last longer than vinyl. Belts should match either your shoes or your pants or skirt. A worn belt will detract from a new suit or pair of slacks. A good-quality pen is essential when writing in front of a business associate. A broken umbrella never makes a good impression.

Also, when you're purchasing clothing, don't forget to accessorize it before you leave the store. Before you can wear the outfit, you may need a scarf, tie or a pair of shoes.

Shoes

Your shoes give others the largest number of clues about your attention to detail and your economic situation. When you leave an interview or meeting, the heels of your shoes are the last thing people see. You've heard the old saying about being "down at the heel." Check your shoes regularly and repair heels before they've completely run down. Use a shoe horn so that the backs of your shoes don't break. Polish them regularly, because in a crisis, polish won't cover deep scuffs that are the result of inattention. When your shoes no longer project a polished image, replace them.

The style of your shoes should be in harmony with the style of your clothes. If your garment is casual, your shoes should be casual. Wearing casual shoes with a formally structured business suit can suggest a lack of awareness. If, for health or comfort, you need to wear specialty footwear, try to obtain comfortable shoes with a more structured look. Now that business casual dress is becoming more common, your choice in this area is wider than before.

To ensure that you make good eye contact with the people you meet, avoid making your shoes so obvious that they become the focal point. The colour of your shoes should either match or be darker than the shade of your hemline. Women can also match the colour of their shoes to their legs. For example, a Caucasian wearing neutral hose can achieve this with a taupe, tan, camel or bone shoe.

Jewellery

Your jewellery works best when it's discreet and of good quality. The exception is if you work in a creative field, where dramatic individuality is usually expected. When it comes to jewellery, less is indeed more, so wear no more than three pieces at once. A bulky sports watch also looks out of place with formal business attire.

Glasses

Glasses not only influence the way you see the world but also affect the way the world views you. In communicating with others, your aim is to draw people's attention to your face and to make good eye contact. Tinted glasses worn indoors will make eye contact difficult and may suggest that you have something to hide. Outdated glasses also become a distraction. They can indicate that you're either unsuccessful or out of touch with the world around you.

Unless you want your frames to make a strong statement, they should complement your face shape, brow line, placement and size of your eyes, length and size of your nose and personal colouring. A slight change in the shape of the frames can make quite a difference to your appearance. An experienced optician has the training to consider all these factors and guide you in your choice of frames.

Glasses are also a communication tool that you can use to your advantage. Pick frames according to your personality and purpose.

What worked for you as a student may not create the desired effect in the business world. Do you want to appear sophisticated or naive? Artistic or scholarly? Authoritative or submissive?

I once had the opportunity to work with a group of law students who were studying non-adversarial approaches to legal proceedings. I asked a student to put on a pair of dark-coloured frames that had a sharp, rectangular shape. He then switched to a medium-coloured, oval-shaped pair. Although both frames suited his face shape, the difference in his appearance was striking.

In the first case, he looked like a severe, urban lawyer, ready to take on a difficult opponent before the Supreme Court. The other frames made him appear less hard-edged and therefore more approachable. This image was more suitable for the small city in which he soon planned to practise law. Tell your optical professional what impression you'd like to make; their advice and expertise can be invaluable.

Clothing Upkeep

Once you have the clothing you need to give you that professional image, taking good care of it will maintain your image. Review your wardrobe regularly in the following areas.

Obvious Lack of Care

There are several image spoilers associated with caring for your clothing.

> • Soiled or unpressed clothing. Beware of the spotted tie or blouse. While natural fibres are more comfortable, except for wool, they crease more and need to be laundered after each wearing.

- Pilled or worn clothing. After extensive wear, areas such as collars and cuffs begin to collect pills (small balls of fibre) or become threadbare. Pills can often be removed by a small electric shaver developed for this purpose. Be especially diligent when you check the collars of your shirts or blouses for wear because they frame your face.

- Light-coloured garments that have gone grey with use or inappropriate laundering.

- Broken or missing buttons.

- Hems falling down. In an emergency, you can use tape, staples or safety pins as a temporary measure. Have the hems repaired at the end of the day, or you may forget and pull the garment out of your closet again.

- Static cling in dry environments. Use a fabric softener or anti-static spray each time you clean a garment to avoid the embarrassment that can come with this problem.

- Don't forget your outer garments, such as coats and raincoats. Regular dry cleaning of light-coloured coats is essential. When you wear a full-length coat, it should come at least two to three inches (5 to 7.5 cm) below your knee if you're wearing pants and two or three inches below the hemline of a skirt or dress.

Invest in a Clothes Brush and Lint Remover

Check your clothes regularly for salt and dried mud stains. Soil caught in the fibres of your clothing acts like glass, eventually cutting it. To prolong the life of your garments, wait until the area is dry, then use a good-quality clothes brush to remove salt and soil. If the salt doesn't disappear, try removing it with a bit of diluted white vinegar after first testing on a hidden area of the garment.

Lint can be distracting, and it affects your professional image. Avoid wearing a down coat with a navy wool suit. The result may leave you either looking like you have a pet that sheds or that you haven't cleaned your suit for years.

Jackets and Travelling

When you travel in an automobile, train, bus or plane, never wear a jacket for any length of time. If you're driving an automobile, the upper arms of the jacket will become deeply creased, and the back will become obviously wrinkled, especially if the day is warm. If you can't hang the jacket on a suit hanger, fold it with the lining to the outside and place it where it won't get crushed. This will not only improve your image but also extend the life of the jacket.

Dry Cleaning

Don't over-clean a constructed garment such as a suit: It quickly causes it to appear worn. If the garment isn't soiled but just needs pressing, ask a tailor or dry cleaner to only press the garment. Always use a dry cleaner that has a good reputation. A suit that is always worn with a shirt or blouse may only need cleaning once or twice a year.

If you're a smoker, be prepared to invest in good-quality clothing that will withstand frequent dry cleaning. You may not notice stale cigarette odour, but it'll invade the personal space of a non-smoker.

Personal Care

Personal grooming is always a sensitive subject, but it can have a great influence on your personal presentation and image. Taking care of your person reveals your attitude to yourself, others and your work.

Hair

Your hair frames your face, so it should be clean and well styled. If you enhance your hair with colour, touch it up regularly to avoid unsightly "roots." An outdated hairstyle shows that you're out of step with the times. A current hairstyle can help you make the transition from student to working professional.

If you've worn a hairstyle for many years, it probably needs updating. Work with an experienced stylist to design a style that flatters your facial features and gives you the image you want to convey. Appropriate hairstyles can balance many prominent features, such as a wide forehead, a long, narrow face, etc.

Thinning hair is always a challenge. Trying to camouflage this by combing a long strand of hair over thinning areas only serves to draw attention to your hair loss. Either keep your hair short and neatly trimmed or consider getting a hair-replacement system. Today's products are difficult to detect and can greatly increase your self-confidence.

You can dress professionally in your dark "power suit" but spoil your image totally by having dandruff sprinkled over your collar and shoulders. Consult an experienced hair-care professional about this problem. Often it's just the result of a dry scalp, which professional shampoos and conditioners can easily correct. Avoid the tendency to scratch your scalp and seek help. If there is a medical reason for your condition, your physician can prescribe a scalp treatment.

Fragrance

Avoid using excessive fragrance in a business setting. Strong aftershave lotions, colognes, deodorants and perfumes will invade others' personal space. Because allergies or asthma can be triggered by even a small amount of fragrance, some workplaces have banned fragrance altogether. It's sensible to go scentless.

Smoking Odours

If you smoke, be aware of smoking odours that cling to your clothes and breath. Allow at least 20 minutes from the time you finish your last cigarette to the time you meet with someone, and if you'll be close to them, eat a breath mint. Air out your clothing after each wearing. This will not only prolong the life of your garments (especially wool garments) but also reduce your dry-cleaning bills.

Personal Hygiene

Showering or bathing every day, and using deodorant, will keep body odour in check. However, in cultures where deodorant isn't used, this may not be an issue.

Pay attention to good oral hygiene. Not brushing and flossing regularly not only leads to expensive dental bills but contributes to bad breath. Similarly, a tooth that needs repair can cause people to back away from you when you open your mouth. Coffee, tea and smoking will discolour your teeth.

Both men and women should consider a good skin-care regime. Cleaning your pores of impurities will reduce blemishes and leave you with a healthy glow. Sunblocks will help you avoid skin discolouration and, of course, the dangers of excessive exposure to the sun.

Fingernails

Your hands play a large role in communication. Nails that are dirty, chipped or misshapen send a message that you neglect small details.

A good manicure will help you avoid unsightly or rough hangnails, which other people will feel when they shake your hand. In a business setting, don't go to extremes with overly long or flashy nails. If you bite your fingernails, try to break the habit, but remember that it takes 21 days to change a behavioural pattern.

Body Piercings and Tattoos

Body piercings and tattoos are very personal expressions of individuality. In most business contexts, it's advisable not to display them because they can create a barrier to communication. If you choose to do so, you must be prepared to accept adverse reactions and rejection.

Chewing and Snapping Gum

Gum chewing and snapping aren't fitting in either business or social settings. If you use gum to freshen your breath, chew it inconspicuously for a few minutes, then remove it and dispose of it discreetly.

Physical Wellness

You can spend a lot of time, energy and money acquiring an incredible wardrobe. However, if you don't have a healthy diet, aren't physically active and ignore the signs of stress, you won't have the substance to realize your image potential.

Nutrition

Your energy level and muscle strength, as well as the colour and texture of your skin, are affected by the food you eat. Combining foods correctly, varying your diet, and drinking enough water are essential to maintain a healthy lifestyle.

If you want to lose weight, research has shown that crash diets work against you in the end. While you follow a slow and steady weight-loss regime, remember that wearing the correct clothing can make you appear taller and automatically more slender. If you're an athlete, you'll have special dietary concerns. If you favour a vegetarian diet, consuming a wide variety of foods over the course of a day is advisable. Consider working with a registered nutritionist to develop an eating plan for your individual needs and lifelong wellness.

Physical Fitness

Besides nutrition, your level of physical activity will also affect your well-being. Physical fitness affects both the body and the mind. A well-tuned, firm body adds to your positive self-image, and this is crucial to managing your image potential. Thirty minutes of aerobic activity three times a week is usually enough to maintain your fitness level. It'll also enhance your health by boosting your energy, calming any anxiety and increasing blood circulation. If you find a physical-fitness regime difficult to establish and maintain, use the services of a personal trainer to help you develop a weekly routine that fits into your schedule.

Stress and Time Management

Stress can play a major role in limiting your image potential. It's also at the root of many debilitating illnesses. Planning your week to include personal time, beyond the demands of your career and family, is an important factor in reducing stress. If you're a well-dressed businessperson who is always late for appointments, you'll compromise your professional image. Include managing priorities in your weekly routine to handle your stress and time concerns, or they'll manage you.

Maximize your potential:
A quality image is tied to the details!

Chapter 7

Men's Image Spoilers

I've written *Managing Your Image Potential* to speak to both men and women. However, on the topic of establishing a quality image, there are certain points that are specific to menswear that need to be covered separately.

Fine-Tuning the Details

An insignificant detail of your attire can interrupt the communication process. A button out of place, a tie that twists, an overcoat that is too short—all these, and more, can create visual distractions. Pay close attention to the following tips.

Short-Sleeved Dress Shirts

A bare (and sometimes hairy) arm peeking out of your jacket sleeve doesn't project a professional image. A long-sleeved dress shirt is always appropriate. If you're warm, wear a long-sleeved shirt, remove your jacket and roll your sleeves halfway to the elbow. A short-sleeved dress shirt worn with a tie doesn't project an image of quality.

Tight Shirt Collars

In effective communication, your face is the focal point, so you want to draw people's eyes there. A collar that is too tight becomes a distraction just short of the mark. The excess flesh that spills over the top of the collar is unsightly, and a collar that is too tight actually cuts off blood circulation to the brain, affecting its function and causing dizziness. Many young men have used cosmetic surgery to repair the visible damage done by wearing a tight collar.

Button-Down Shirt Collars

Never wear a shirt with a button-down collar with a double-breasted jacket. Double-breasted jackets tend to look more formal, while button-down collars are more sporty. If you enjoy the neat appearance that button-down collars create, purchase shirts that have hidden snap or button closures beneath the collar points.

Buttoning Jackets and Vests

A double-breasted jacket should be buttoned when you're standing and unbuttoned when you're sitting down. (In fact, most jackets are more comfortable when you unbutton them before you sit down.) When you wear a single-breasted jacket with anywhere from two to five buttons, *never button the bottom button!* With a three-button jacket, you can button the top two buttons, a single button at the middle or just the top one.

Never button the bottom button on a vest. This tradition may stem from the story that Edward VII, while Prince of Wales, inadvertently left the bottom button on his waistcoat undone. Everyone followed suit to avoid embarrassment (Keers 1988, 34). A practical reason for keeping the bottom button undone, however, is to prevent the creasing that naturally occurs when you're sitting down.

Suit Jackets versus Blazers

A suit jacket is meant to be worn with its matching pants. It's usually cut a little tighter than a blazer or sports jacket. If you try to use it in place of a blazer with contrasting trousers, you won't achieve a natural, balanced look. If you regularly wear your suit trousers without the jacket, the trousers will wear out long before the jacket does. The solution is to purchase either two pairs of trousers (this can be arranged by a quality menswear retailer) or separate trousers to wear on more casual days.

If your thighs are heavy, causing your slacks to wear quickly, ask a tailor or the retailer where you purchase them to line them to the knee and reinforce the crotch.

Overcoats

Look for an overcoat that is long enough, especially if you're taller than average. Full-length coats should come at least two to three inches below your knee. If you prefer to wear a shorter overcoat, choose a three-quarter-length coat rather than a short bomber jacket, which won't be long enough to cover your suit coat.

Tie Tips

Your tie is a very important expression of your personality. Here are some tips for using it to your best advantage.

> • Tie your tie with a tight knot so that the narrow end is shorter than the wide end. Then tuck the narrow end into the tab on the reverse side of the wide end.

Managing Your Image Potential

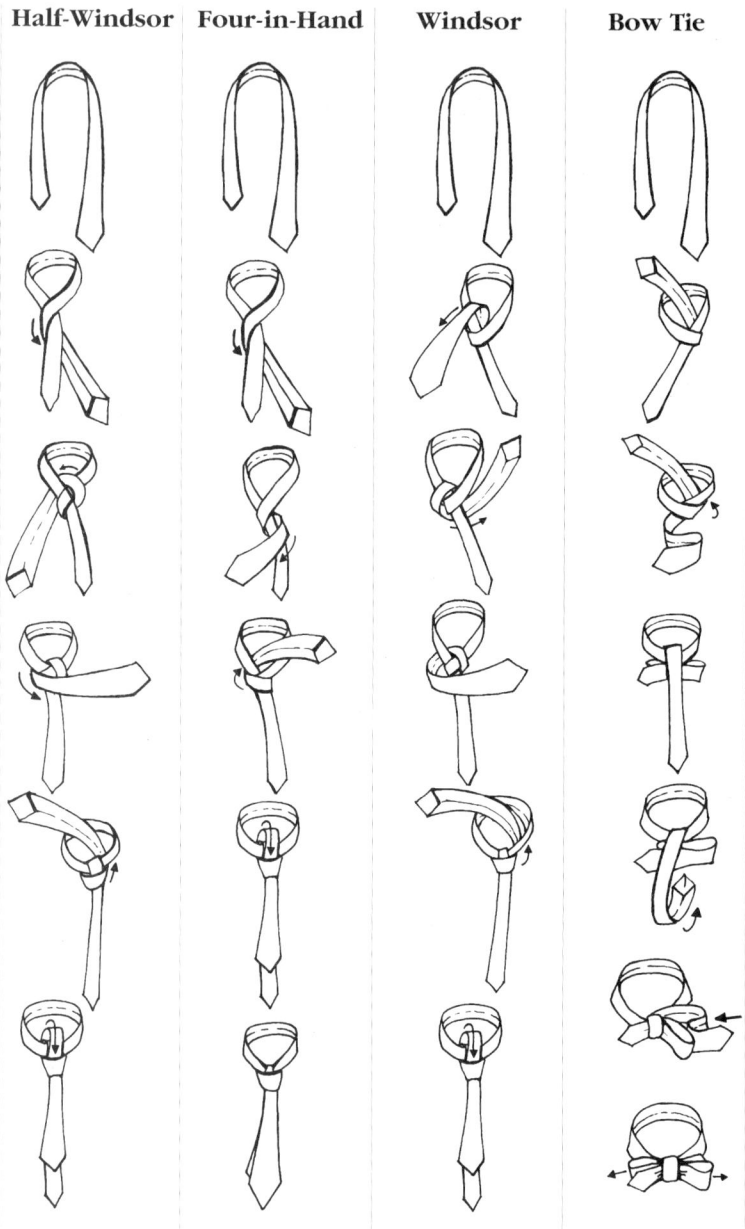

- If the narrow end of your tie is too short to tuck into the tab, never tuck it between the top two buttons of your shirt. It'll distort the knot and become distracting. Ask your tailor to move the tab up.

- There should always be one or more dimples in your tie at the base of the knot. This helps the tie spread and prevents it from collapsing and looking like a rope.

- Your tie should always reach your belt buckle. It shouldn't end above or below the belt.

- Ensure that the knot fills the space between your collar points. A four-in-hand knot isn't expected to fill the space of a wide-spread collar. A Windsor knot is usually too bulky for a button-down or pinned collar.

- If you have a wide, short neck, a four-in-hand knot will create length. To wear a bow tie, your neck must be long. Bow ties aren't usually worn for business.

- If either your chest or lower body is more prominent than the other, the pattern and texture of your ties can affect the balance between them. If you're small, don't overpower yourself with a tie in a large, loud pattern.

- The width of your tie should be close to the width of the lapel on your jacket.

- When you wear a blazer, your tie can be in a bolder pattern or colour than when you wear a suit. Fashion trends and your clothing personality also influence your tie patterns.

- Purchase good-quality ties. Hold the tie by the small end and see if it hangs straight. If it twists, it's not cut on the true bias, and it'll always twist on your body. The tie should be interfaced with pure wool and loosely stitched at the tips of both ends to allow for some movement as you knot it. Ties should be fully lined.

• At the end of the day, always loosen the knot and untie your tie completely. Don't pull the knot down and slip the tie over your head. In time, you'll break the stitching on the back. If the tie has become excessively creased, place both ends together and roll the tie up as you would a belt. The creases are usually gone by morning.

• Once soiled, many ties cannot be cleaned successfully and should be replaced.

The Wandering Waistband

Some men prefer to wear the waistband of their pants low in the front. If this is you, have your pants altered at the waistband to remove length. If the front drops too low, it can affect your general appearance. Using suspenders to bring the waistline parallel to the floor is always correct. It'll also make it easier to have the end of your tie somewhere within the waistband area.

Beware of waistbands that are too tight. Research done by Dr. Octavio Bessa, a veteran internist in Stamford, Connecticut, has attributed certain gastrointestinal problems to Tight Pants Syndrome, or TPS (Zezima 1995). Symptoms such as vague abdominal discomfort, distention (at times radiating to the chest), heartburn and frequent belching have been traced to pants that are too tight. Bessa has concluded that 90 per cent of men suffer from TPS. To avoid such discomfort, a good tailor can help you select your correct waistband size and, if necessary, alter the seat of your pants.

Stuffed Pockets

Carrying too much in your pockets will distort and damage your garments. Consider putting your overstuffed wallet in a briefcase or portfolio, or distributing the contents among different pockets in your clothing. Carrying a purse is common in Europe, although not in North America.

Socks

Ensure that your dress socks are long enough to cover your leg when you're sitting down. Over-the-calf socks in a colour that matches your shoes or pants are best. Avoid white or brightly coloured socks for business.

Maximize your potential:
Check every detail from head to toe!

Chapter 8

Women's Image Spoilers

Over the past several years, numerous studies have shown that there are more men than women in top executive positions and that women continue to earn less than men. There are numerous reasons for this, including the years women choose to take from their careers to have children and priorities that involve a shorter work week so they can spend time with their families.

Polish Your Professional Image

Image also plays a huge role in whether a woman gets ahead in her career. Use the following points to polish your professional image and give you an advantage over the competition.

Jacket Power

As mentioned in the chapter on wardrobe communication, a 1993 study showed that a woman wearing a jacket was perceived to have more power than a woman who didn't. In this study, respondents didn't perceive any difference between a jacket worn with a skirt (as a suit) and a jacket worn over a dress.

Keep in mind that your appearance will be more formal (and more powerful) if your jacket matches your dress than if you wear it with a contrasting dress. Thus, wearing a navy jacket over a navy dress will be stronger than wearing a navy jacket over a tan dress.

Shoes

Open-toed shoes and sandals aren't considered appropriate for business. Closed-toed pumps with medium, tapered heels are always appropriate. Slingback shoes are also acceptable. The longer the skirt, the higher the heel can be. Spike heels aren't recommended for business.

It's traditional in North America to wear white shoes in the summer months. This is only appropriate if you're wearing a garment that is mainly white. When you wear white shoes with a darker garment, you not only make your feet appear larger, but you also create a focal point at your feet instead of your face.

Hosiery

Always wear hosiery in a business context. During the warmer months of the year, hosiery made from microfibres is a cooler option. Neutral hosiery, one or two tones deeper than your skin tone, is always correct. Other shades such as black, charcoal, grey and navy are also acceptable if they coordinate with the colours of your shoes and hemline. Matching the colour of your hose, shoes and hemline will elongate your legs.

Textured and patterned hose will shorten your legs, while opaque or dark hose will make them appear thinner. If you don't want the contours of your legs to be obvious, don't wear opaque hose. Never wear light-coloured hose, such as white or bone, with dark shoes.

Having runs in your hosiery is a definite image spoiler. Nail polish can only repair a small, hidden run. Keep an extra pair of hose in the colour(s) you frequently wear in your desk, car or briefcase.

Skirts

The length of your skirt should be in keeping with its style and your vertical proportions. If you have long legs, you have a greater range of skirt lengths than someone with short legs. To avoid looking heavier in the hip area, ensure that your skirt is always longer than it is wide when the waistband is showing.

In a business setting, skirts should be no shorter than two to three inches above the knee. Skirts that are slit too high or are too tight can be revealing and distracting and will usually limit your movements. If you wear a straight skirt with a slit, the slit should be worn at the back. If your skirt is unlined, remember to wear a slit slip to ensure that the slip remains concealed.

Pants versus Skirts

In some conventional businesses and certain geographical areas, women who wear skirts or dresses are judged to be more professional than those who wear pants. Observe other women in your work environment to learn what seems to be expected. For some women, a skirt isn't an appropriate option at any time. To lessen possible discrimination, wear pants with a matching jacket, preferably in a dark colour.

Shoulder Pads

Many women will remove shoulder pads from a garment before wearing it. Structured jackets usually depend on a shoulder pad to fit and drape correctly. If the shoulder pads are too large for you (the collar rises from the back of your neck, and horizontal folds appear in the shoulder area), don't remove the pads entirely; instead, ask a tailor to reduce their depth. Some women with sloped shoulders will notice diagonal creases at the bottom of the armholes of their garments. Using slightly larger shoulder pads will correct this. If you have a full bust, full waist, full hip or full figure, shoulder pads can also create balance.

Purses and Briefcases

Avoid carrying a purse and a briefcase at the same time. When you need to shake hands with someone, you don't want to be fumbling to move both of them out of the way. If you carry a briefcase in one hand and have a shoulder bag over your shoulder on the same side, you may find that the purse will slip off your shoulder and fall to the ground.

Revealing and Sleeveless Garments

In a business setting, cover your upper arms; sleeveless garments belong to the relaxed business casual level of dress. The necklines of your garments shouldn't be cut so low as to be revealing. If a blouse is semi-transparent, wear a camisole and bra that are close to your skin tone. A black or coloured bra beneath a white blouse is a definite image spoiler. A top that is completely transparent isn't appropriate either.

"Busting Out"

If the placement of buttons on a blouse or dress doesn't allow for one near the bust, ask a dressmaker or tailor to sew on an invisible snap. This will prevent the front of the item from gaping. Make sure that your garments have adequate room in the bust. This is especially important when you wear a jacket. If the jacket is too tight over your bust, the jacket will tend to gape, and you'll be constantly tugging it back to its intended position. Not only is this activity a nuisance to you, it simply draws more attention to your bust.

Fabric Watch

What is appropriate in one region may not be appropriate in another. For example, in large urban centres, you'll look more professional in silk blouses than in sweaters and polyester blouses; wool is also preferred to synthetics in suits, unless they are made from fine microfibres. If you want to project a powerful image in a business setting, floral patterns (especially in light colours) and lace fabrics aren't suitable for major wardrobe pieces.

You can negatively affect your professional image by choosing garments in shiny fabrics. Women's clothing is often made from these fabrics, and although the style of a garment may be tailored, the character of the fabric moves the garment from the category of business attire to dressy. Garments in these fabrics are also a poor investment because they don't stand up to repeated dry cleaning.

Makeup

Whether to wear makeup or not is a personal decision. If your skin has an uneven tone, applying foundation can camouflage the differences in colour and texture. Wearing a small amount of makeup can give you a more mature and polished image. For the office, keep makeup to a minimum and always make sure it's flattering to your colouring.

Maximize your potential:
Use jackets to your advantage!

Chapter 9

Planning Your Wardrobe

You'll always reap great benefits from planning. If you take an organized approach to acquiring your clothing instead of buying garments on the spur of the moment, you'll save time, energy and money. This chapter addresses choosing classic styles, coordinating textures and patterns, taking an inventory of your closet, buying quality and building wardrobe modules that will give you lots of options.

Choosing Timeless Classics

Classic clothes have a timeless appeal. These designs were created in the past, and they're still worn successfully today. Classics aren't necessarily basic in terms of the garment details. Take, for instance, a man's Norfolk jacket (Keers 1988, 36). This interesting jacket, which has a loose, comfortable fit with a belt, box pleats and patch pockets, evokes country life in the British Isles, where the style originated on the Duke of Norfolk's estate. Other classic styles such as turtleneck sweaters, navy blazers and straight skirts are more basic in appearance.

Although the essential details of a classic garment are traditional, its general fit may change over a long period of time. For instance, jackets in the 1970s had a much tighter fit and a higher armhole than those 30 years later. Menswear moves more slowly than womenswear, so a man can usually wear a classic garment for a longer period of time. However, beware of keeping a classic garment in your closet after its cut no longer bears any resemblance to garments in the stores.

Mixing Classics with Fashion

When your wardrobe consists of only classics, it can appear drab. When you build your wardrobe, choose classic pieces in traditional colours for the higher-investment items such as suits and coats, then bring in some fashion colours using lower-priced shirts, blouses, sweaters, ties and scarves. This strategy will help you maintain a contemporary look and ultimately maximize your clothing dollar.

Coordinating Textures and Patterns

When you combine different pieces in your wardrobe, you must strive to coordinate the textures and patterns. Although some textural contrast is interesting, it's safe to suggest that if you keep similar fabric textures together, the result will be pleasing to the eye and the touch. And if all your garments are in the same colour, you can create very effective textural contrast.

For example, a good combination would include a tweed jacket, a pair of corduroy slacks, an oxford cloth shirt and a woven wool scarf or tie. These fabrics all have surface interest often associated with a casual wardrobe. At the opposite end of the scale would be a hard-finished, worsted wool suit, a Sea Island cotton shirt or a silk blouse plus a silk tie or scarf. These smoother fabrics have a more formal look. If in the first outfit with the tweed jacket, you replaced the oxford cloth shirt with a shiny, silk one in a contrasting colour, the two fabric textures wouldn't work as well as a silk shirt with a matte finish.

Another example using womenswear would be a casual, cotton suit worn with a shiny, stretch lace top. The suit would have a dull appearance and would probably look better with a T-shirt or cotton-knit top that isn't as dressy as the lace top.

When you combine patterns, the safe route is to follow the guideline "Less is more." When you're wearing a suit, shirt and tie, always choose at least one piece in a plain fabric. For example, a pinstriped suit with a patterned tie would be best worn with a plain shirt. It takes an expert eye to combine three patterned items. You can do this successfully either when the colour scheme is monochromatic or when the pattern of the fabric in one piece is so subtle that from a distance, it looks like a solid colour.

Taking a Closet Inventory

Before you can plan your wardrobe, you need to look at what you already own and compare it with your lifestyle needs. If you're a student who's about to enter the business world and you've been wearing jeans and sweatshirts for the past few years, expect to have new demands placed on your wardrobe. Do you have items in your closet that can take you to your first interview and beyond? How much time will you spend dressed casually? What percentage of your week will you need to dress in work attire? How often will you need to dress formally?

Think about the clothes you wear more than once a week. Why do you enjoy wearing them? Is it the colour, the texture or the style that makes them your favourites? These styles should become essential items in your basic wardrobe because comfort is also an essential factor in wardrobe building. If you're not comfortable in a garment, you won't enjoy wearing it and will tend to leave it buried in your closet.

With these factors in mind, take a close look at the apparel in your closet and put each item into one of the following categories:

1. Items to keep that:

- require no alterations to achieve good fit or proportion
- match your personality and lifestyle
- are comfortable to wear
- are in keeping with current fashion trends
- are in good condition
- are your "fun" or sentimental clothes

2. Items to keep that need:

- repairing (missing buttons, hems falling down, etc.)
- cleaning
- altering (lengthening, shortening, taking in or out)
- advice from an image professional to see if they can be improved
- another piece or some accessories to complete the outfit before you can wear it

3. Items to be given away because they:

- are too small
- don't fit your personality (all those gift items!)

- are out of style
- haven't been worn for the past three years
- are worn or stained
- no longer fit your lifestyle needs

Budgeting

Spend your clothing dollars where you spend your time. If your closet is currently filled with nothing but casual clothing and a change in your lifestyle or career requires you to have a corporate wardrobe, plan to acquire work-related items. If you'll be spending 70 per cent of your time in work clothes, approximately 70 per cent of your wardrobe should consist of styles suitable for work. Be careful not to buy something you don't need just because it's on sale. A garment that you don't wear is the most expensive piece in your closet, whatever you paid for it.

A higher-quality garment may cost you more initially; however, the construction and fabric usually allow you to wear it for a longer period of time than a lower-priced garment. This reduces the garment's cost per wearing dramatically. When you choose a garment that you hope to wear for five to six years, select a classic piece that, unlike a fad or hot fashion trend, won't look dated after one or two seasons.

Natural fabrics, especially wool, will last far longer than blends of polyester and viscose or polyester and acetate. If you have an aversion to wool because it's scratchy, it may be that you've only tried the coarser, less expensive types. Higher-quality wool fibres are extremely smooth to the touch. Cool wool can also be worn year round, making it even more cost-effective.

Tailored garments that have interfacing and lining, and those made in fibres such as wool and rayon, require dry cleaning. Remember to include the cost of dry cleaning in your budget.

Analyzing the Cost per Wearing

Before buying an article of clothing, analyze the cost per wearing by dividing its cost by the total number of times you'll wear it.

$$\text{Cost per wearing} = \frac{\text{Cost of garment (including upkeep)}}{\text{Total number of wearings}}$$

To arrive at the *Total number of wearings,* follow this calculation:

Number of wearings per week
x
Approximate number of weeks in a month (4)
x
Number of months in the year that you can wear the garment
x
Number of years that you can wear the garment
=
Total number of wearings

The costing example below shows that the cool wool suit costs more than double the jacket and pants outfit ($600.00 compared to $175.00 + $100.00 = $275.00); however, its cost per wearing ($1.50) is a third less than the other two pieces combined ($2.24).

Costing Example

This example shows that the number of months per year that you can wear a garment greatly affects the cost of your wardrobe.

Planning Your Wardrobe: Costing Example

	Cool Wool Suit	Linen-Blend Jacket	Polyester & Viscose Pants
Cost	$600.00	$175.00	$100.00
Number of wearings per week	2	2	3
Number of weeks per month	4	4	4
Number of months it can be worn per year	10	4	10
Number of years it can be worn	5	3	2
Total number of wearings	400	96	240
Cost per wearing	$1.50	$1.82	$0.42

Your wardrobe will also be versatile if it's transitional, which means you can wear it all year. You can only wear the linen jacket four months of the year because the fibre is associated with warmer weather. The polyester and viscose in the pants is a good year-round fabric, but it'll begin to pill and look worn after the first year. You can wear cool wool at least 10 months of the year, and in an air-conditioned environment, 12 months. Aim to have at least 75 per cent of your wardrobe in transitional fabrics and colours.

Both jackets will require dry cleaning, which adds to their cost. The linen jacket will crease easily and not look as polished and professional as a jacket in wool. Although the seperate pants and jacket appear to be a more economical purchase initially, the wool suit is obviously a better investment.

Building Wardrobe Modules

When you examine the pieces in your closet, do you see a wardrobe that has been developed to mix and match harmoniously, or do you see items that were unique when you purchased them and remain "orphans" in your closet because they don't coordinate with anything? When your clothing dollar is limited, it makes sense to plan your purchases to achieve a wardrobe that will work for you. One way to do this is to build wardrobe modules.

A wardrobe module is a small group of items in one or two colours that you can wear together. Nine pieces of well-coordinated clothing will create 20 outfits. Such an approach not only makes getting dressed easier but also simplifies packing for a trip and building your first working wardrobe on a tight budget.

General Guidelines

- Identify the lifestyle criteria that the module must meet. Is it to be a working wardrobe or a casual one? Do you need items that can satisfy several lifestyle needs?

- Choose two basic colours. The best colours suit your personal colouring and can be worn together. You'll be wearing these colours frequently, so choose basic colours such as black, navy, bone and/or taupe that you won't tire of easily. Brighter fashion colours are best kept as accents.

- Using your wardrobe inventory, select a core garment. A favourite jacket, skirt or pair of pants is a good place to start. Decide on a basic colour.

- Complete one outfit by choosing companion garments for the core item. For instance, if the core garment is a jacket, you'll need pants or a skirt plus a shirt, blouse or sweater

Planning Your Wardrobe: Building Wardrobe Modules

to create an outfit. If the bottom you choose is in the same colour as the jacket, you'll achieve a "suited look." An example of casual companion pieces would be a pair of jeans, a denim jacket and a T-shirt.

• Repeat this procedure to complete another outfit, working in the second basic colour. You may want to choose a subtle check or stripe in this grouping. Take special care to ensure that you can wear the pieces of this second outfit with those of the first. For example, if the first outfit is in navy and the second basic colour is taupe, you can wear the taupe bottom with the navy jacket and vice versa. Two "suits" that can intermix form the basis of a wardrobe module.

For men, the companion garments you must work with are sports coats and trousers, not full suits. Usually, you cannot disassemble and remix the pieces of a structured suit. See "Suit Jackets versus Blazers" in the chapter on men's image spoilers. If a more casual wardrobe is your goal, exchange the jackets for vests or cardigans.

• Add three more tops, another bottom and a pullover or cardigan that will coordinate with these outfits. If you want a more casual look, consider using sweaters. These items can be in accent or fashion colours to add spice to the basics.

• Decide what you'll need in accessories to coordinate with the garments: shoes, hosiery, belts, scarves, ties, jewellery, purses, briefcases, portfolios, etc. These pieces can add life and interest to your basic wardrobe module. By changing your accessories, you can totally alter your appearance. When you purchase accessories, learn to select quality, not quantity.

This wardrobe module will become one "corner" of your wardrobe. The guidelines above include nine pieces: two jackets, three bottoms, three tops and one sweater to create 20 outfits. Add three more tops, and you'll be able to build 40 outfits.

The next step is to assemble a second module that coordinates with at least half of the first grouping. For instance, you can take the taupe pieces from the first module and mix them with red, forest green or black.

Basic Module for Men

The following is an initial nine-piece wardrobe module that is suitable if you're a man working in an environment where the dress is tailored business casual. You're not expected to wear a matched suit to work every day, but you often need a jacket.

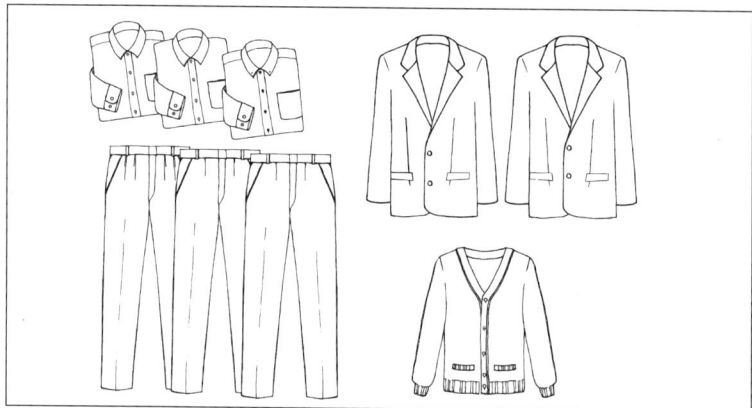

- 2 blazers or sports coats (solids or subtle patterns)

- 3 pairs of trousers that will coordinate with both the blazers and sports coats

- 3 shirts (neutrals and colours in both smooth and subtle

textures that will coordinate with all the jackets and trousers)

• 1 sweater (a mock turtleneck, polo shirt or full turtleneck that can go under the jackets or a pullover or cardigan to coordinate with the above shirts and trousers)

Over time, I suggest that you add about seven more shirts or sweaters that can go under the jackets, one classic suit for more formal occasions and a trench coat.

Basic Accessories

- 6 ties
- 2 pairs of leather shoes (black, oxblood)
- 2 leather belts to match shoes
- 10 pairs of socks (over-the-calf) to match shoes
- 1 leather portfolio
- 1 leather briefcase or attaché case
- classic, understated jewellery (watch, ring)

Basic Module for Women

The following is an initial nine-piece wardrobe module that is suitable if you're a woman working in an environment where you're expected to wear a matched suit to work every day.

• 2 cool wool or microfibre polyester suits in coordinating textures and basic colours that you can mix and match (solids or subtle patterns in classic colours such as navy, black, mid-grey, burgundy, deep purple or forest green)

• 1 more skirt or pair of pants that can coordinate with both suit jackets

- 3 shirts or blouses (plain colours and subtle patterns that coordinate with all the above pieces)

- 1 sweater (crewneck, mock turtleneck or full turtleneck that can go under the jackets or a pullover or cardigan to coordinate with the above pieces)

To avoid having to do laundry twice a week and to increase the life of your garments, I suggest that you add about seven more shirts, blouses or sweaters that can go under the jackets. Other useful additions to this wardrobe are a microfibre all-weather trench coat and either a dress that can go under some of the jackets or a coat dress that can double as a suit.

Basic Accessories

- 2 pairs of shoes (closed-toed pumps, loafers, slingbacks)
- 1 good-quality leather handbag
- 1 leather belt

- 1 leather portfolio
- 1 leather briefcase or attaché case
- scarves
- pantyhose
- classic, understated jewellery (hoop earrings, watch, rings)

Developing your wardrobe in this manner reaps tremendous rewards. For example, if one garment is being cleaned or needs ironing, there will always be something else in your closet that you can wear in its place. It also allows you to pack quickly for a sudden business trip. It helps in the "crisis dressing" that occurs when you haven't decided what you're going to wear the next day and wake up to find that your alarm didn't go off. When you have 20 minutes to get ready for an important meeting and you need to look your best, you can quickly reach into your closet and pull together an appropriate outfit from your module pieces. Finally, you can wear your clothing with confidence, knowing that all your garments and accessories look good—and so do you.

Maximize your potential:
Use wardrobe planning strategies!

Chapter 10

Fabric Characteristics and Care

Gaining some elementary knowledge of the characteristics of textile fibres will make you a better-informed fashion consumer. This chapter provides reference lists of the favourable and unfavourable characteristics of the most popular clothing fibres, along with some basic care information.

Natural Fibres

Cotton

Favourable

- good strength, 10 per cent stronger when wet
- good resistance to abrasion
- absorbs moisture, making it cool and comfortable
- no static or pilling

Unfavourable

- dull appearance
- wrinkles
- no elasticity (doesn't retain shape in knits)
- attacked by mildew and silverfish

Care

- machine-wash and -dry; can be dry cleaned
- use chlorine bleach only on white fabrics

Linen

Favourable

- excellent strength (twice as strong as cotton) and 10 per cent stronger when wet
- very absorbent
- good wicking action (removes moisture to the outside of the garment)
- no static or pilling

Unfavourable

- poor drape, stiff
- wrinkles easily
- fair resistance to abrasion (breaks if folded in one position for a long time)
- attacked by mildew and silverfish

Care

- machine-wash or dry clean
- dampen and iron at a high temperature
- don't use too much chlorine bleach

Silk

Favourable

- very strong
- resists wrinkles
- excellent drape, luxurious hand, lustrous
- absorbs moisture (comfortable, dries quickly, gives up soil in washing)
- little static; no pilling

Unfavourable

- fair resistance to abrasion
- loses 15 per cent strength when wet
- poor resistance to sunlight and perspiration
- attacked by moths

Care

- wash or dry clean (a particular dye or finish sometimes requires dry cleaning only)
- don't bleach (yellows with chlorine bleach)
- iron at a medium-high setting (turns yellow at high temperatures)

Wool

Favourable

- wrinkles hang out, especially in a moist atmosphere
- garments hold their shape
- provides warmth without weight
- cool in warm weather (especially lightweight cool wools)

- the most absorbent fibre, but feels dry when full of water
- naturally extinguishes flame
- tailors well

Unfavourable

- loses 25 per cent of its strength when wet
- shrinks if washed in hot water or if agitated too much in cold water
- prone to pilling
- attacked by moths
- can be uncomfortable against the skin

Care

- dry clean, especially woven fabrics and structured garments like jackets
- handwash knitwear in cold water using mild soap and little agitation; rinse well, remove water by rolling in a towel or using the gentle spin-dry cycle of the machine; dry flat away from heat or sun
- don't bleach (yellows with chlorine bleach)

Synthetic Fibres

Many people avoid synthetics because their texture isn't always pleasant against the skin. In addition, synthetics' inability to wick away moisture makes people feel warm. *Microfibres*, which are a lot smaller in diameter than ordinary synthetic fibres, were developed to solve these problems. They're produced mainly from rayon, nylon and polyester.

Fabric Characteristics and Care: Synthetic fibres

Acetate

Favourable

- excellent drape and luxurious hand
- no pilling; little static
- resistant to mildew and insects

Unfavourable

- poor strength (30 per cent poorer when wet)
- poor resistance to abrasion
- warm fibre; doesn't wick away moisture (makes a person feel clammy)
- sometimes fades from exposure to atmospheric gas

Care

- dry clean or carefully wash by hand
- may shrink excessively
- creases become permanent at high temperatures

Acrylic

Favourable

- lightweight; good drape
- wool-like hand; warm
- doesn't wrinkle
- excellent resistance to sunlight and weathering
- doesn't stain easily

Unfavourable

- elasticity varies widely

- fair strength; 20 per cent weaker when wet
- doesn't absorb water, causing static and pilling
- fair resistance to abrasion

Care

- machine-wash; colours stay bright after many washings
- don't use hot water, or wrinkles become permanent; dry knitwear on a cool to medium setting; a hot dryer causes a garment to stretch and lose its shape

Nylon

Favourable

- lightweight and very strong
- high resistance to abrasion
- good elasticity and resiliency
- excellent drape
- smooth (stains wipe off)

Unfavourable

- doesn't absorb water well, causing static and pilling
- poor resistance to sunlight and mildew

Care

- washes well, but dye transfers from other garments that aren't colourfast

Polyester

Favourable

- very good strength and resistance to abrasion
- doesn't wrinkle; keeps its shape

- resistant to mildew and pests
- good resistance to sunlight behind glass
- dries rapidly

Unfavourable

- absorbs very little moisture, causing static and pilling
- oil stains fabric easily, and it's difficult to remove the oil
- absorbs and holds body odours

Care

- best wash-and-wear fibre
- dry cleaning can sometimes remove oil stains
- iron on a low setting, or it'll melt

Polypropylene (Olefin)

Favourable

- the lightest, warmest fibre
- high strength; good resistance to abrasion
- excellent resistance to sunlight and weather
- excellent resiliency
- excellent wicking action in microfibre form (sports socks and underwear)
- resists perspiration, rot, mildew, staining, insects

Unfavourable

- doesn't absorb water (to overcome this, it's often mixed with other fibres)
- has static
- the surface texture is unpleasant (rough)

Care

- iron, wash and dry at low temperatures

Rayon/Viscose

Favourable

- absorbs moisture; no static or pilling
- excellent drape, soft, pliable
- can make a fine, sheer, strong fabric

Unfavourable

- weaker than cotton
- loses 30 to 70 per cent of its strength when wet
- stretches and wrinkles
- can shrink each time it's washed if the fibre hasn't been treated
- attacked by mildew and silverfish

Care

- follow the care label carefully
- mostly dry clean, but some garments can be gently washed by hand
- hang to dry

Caring for and Storing Clothing

Buying a wardrobe is an investment in your future. You can spend a lot of money on quality garments that should last you a long time, but if you don't care for and store them properly, you'll need to replace them sooner than you anticipate.

Brushing and Airing Frequently

Brushing and airing your clothes will keep them looking good and make them last longer.

- Brush napped surfaces regularly; this removes dust and soil, which cut fibres. Wait for the soil to dry and then use a soft, firm bristle brush to remove it. This treatment is good for garments that you can't wash, such as wool.

- Air your garments after you wear them; this offsets perspiration absorption, removes odours and prolongs the life of wool garments.

- Button or zip up garments and hang them either in a well-ventilated closet without crushing them, or on a hook or line away from direct sunlight.

- Use padded hangers.

Removing Stains Immediately

Always remove stains as quickly as possible using the correct method.

- Don't allow stains to set.

- Never use hot water on an unknown stain because it can set it.

- Remove greasy stains using dry cleaning fluid (you can also try talcum powder to remove hot butter).

- Different fibres require different methods (refer to a stain-removal handbook).

- Remove stains before cleaning a garment.

Storing for the Season

Before storing garments at the end of a season, follow these guidelines to ensure that your clothing looks just as good when you go to wear it again.

- Clean garments first; stains will oxidize and become permanent, and insects will be attracted to the fibres. Insects will actually eat through unappetizing synthetic fibres to enjoy any food that may have dropped onto a garment.

- Store garments in dust-proof containers; include a moth preventive with wools.

- Never store cotton or linen garments in contact with raw wood or wood finishes in drawers or closets because their cellulose fibres will yellow when they come into contact with the acids in wood and its finishes.

- Wash newly purchased linens to remove the starch in the sizing, which can encourage mildew and silverfish.

- Refold linen from time to time, or the fibres will eventually break.

- Remove any pins, which will cause rust stains.

- Use cloth bags instead of plastic to store your clothing. The acids in the plastic will discolour garments. Plastic also traps moisture (mildew) and attracts dust, which cuts the fibres.

Mending Immediately

Mending clothing immediately prevents further damage.

- Repair broken seams or tears; wearing a garment with pins, etc. can cause further damage.

- Repair a garment before laundering it because the tear can become larger.

Using the Correct Cleaning Method

Cleaning your garments correctly prolongs their life and makes them always look their best.

Washing

- You can wash cotton, linen and most rayons.
- Wash garments promptly after wearing them, especially if you've worn them next your skin.
- Remove bad stains first.
- If a garment is very soiled, first soak it for ten minutes in warm, sudsy water.
- Never use very hot water.
- Be careful with bleach: If you use too much, cotton will yellow; wool and silk will always yellow.
- Softeners remove static but decrease absorbency; avoid using them on active sportswear, which needs to absorb perspiration.
- Use the proper method for the garment: hand, machine, gentle, permanent press, etc.

Dry Cleaning

- Dry cleaning wool prevents shrinkage. But don't over-clean wool; if a garment is only wrinkled, have it pressed.
- Removes grease spots from polyester.
- Doesn't always remove body odour.

Ironing or Pressing Properly

Understanding when to iron and when to press will keep your garments looking professional.

- Pressing is used on wool and delicate fibres: The iron is used in an up-and-down motion rather than the vigorous back-and-forth movement of ironing.
- Use a press cloth between the garment and the iron on fabrics that will shine.
- Press from the wrong side to prevent the fabric from shining.
- Follow the temperature guide on the iron.
- Iron linen and cotton.

Allowing Rest Periods

Don't wear your clothing two days in a row. If you give your garments a rest between wearings, they'll last longer. This also applies to shoes.

Maximize your potential:
Become an informed fashion consumer!

Chapter 11

Etiquette: Method in Your Manners

Over the years, I've conducted many seminars on business and social etiquette, and I've always made a point of clarifying the difference between etiquette and manners. *Etiquette* is a term that conjures up many unpleasant associations for people. Just mentioning the word can cause a cold chill to fill the room, and everyone can suddenly look embarrassed and confused. I hope that *Managing Your Image Potential* will help change conventional attitudes toward etiquette by adding new perspectives on dining, making introductions, participating in meetings, handling e-mail and cellular telephones, hosting events, announcing your pregnancy at work and so on.

Proper Etiquette Puts You at Ease

Etiquette involves strictly following rules of social behaviour that have evolved over many centuries. If you've asked a client to lunch and you aren't sure which fork to use, you won't be relaxed or confident. However, knowing the rules of etiquette will certainly put you at ease and allow you to concentrate on the business at hand.

There are differences between social and business etiquette. In a social setting, when a person enters a room to meet a group of seated people, it's common practice for the women present to remain seated and shake hands with the newcomer, while the men rise and shake hands. In a business context, however, everyone, regardless of gender, should rise and greet the newcomer.

In business, etiquette doesn't follow gender-determined principles. Everyone is on an equal footing, and distinctions are determined only by rank and position. Because social and business norms are constantly evolving, it's essential to keep current about these changes. No one likes a social dinosaur.

Good Manners Give You Power

Manners, on which I prefer to focus, transcend to some extent the rigidity of etiquette. Manners have to do with how the rules of etiquette are applied. Adopting a mannerly attitude puts you in the enviable position of showing consideration for others and their welfare, even to the point of bending a rule of etiquette. It's always wise to learn the rules before you can interpret them and, if need be, break them.

The following story illustrates this point. Apparently, a royal personage was hosting a dinner to which many dignitaries were invited. After the main course was cleared away, individual finger bowls were brought to the table. Without waiting for the host to act first, a guest mistakenly picked up their finger bowl and proceeded to drink the warm liquid. So as not to embarrass the guest, the royal host drank from their bowl as well. Everyone else then followed suit. If the guest had been told that the bowl was for cleaning fingers, he or she would have been embarrassed. The host bent rules of etiquette to show good manners.

Using good manners isn't a sign of weakness: When all else is equal, this skill will set you apart from others. Your demeanour during a job interview can be the deciding factor that tips the scales in your favour, and good manners will make you a valued employee. Many high-powered executives manage with brute force and ignorance, but think of the lost time caused by employees brooding over an impolite remark. Rudeness doesn't show power and assertiveness, just rudeness.

Good manners in any setting are potent motivators that cannot be overlooked. Making politeness a professional and personal policy will set you at ease and fill you with confidence. A moment of kindness can be a transforming experience for you as the giver as well as for the receiver. Respecting others is true power.

In an article that appeared in *The Washington Post*, Reshma Memon Yaqub quoted Dorothea Johnson, CEO of the renowned Protocol School of Washington, on the importance of business etiquette.

> Naysayers equate [etiquette] with insincerity and phoniness. They consider it a hindrance to the bottom line. But in fact, "etiquette has strong, financial impact. Your manners affect your job and the bottom line of your company. We are judged far more than we realize; by our bosses, our co-workers, our clients, our competition."
>
> Rather than impeding the business process, the myriad rules of etiquette actually enhance it. "When you practise proper etiquette, you are practising respect for yourself and for those around you. It keeps individuals within certain boundaries of self-discipline. It creates an atmosphere of reciprocity. They say good guys finish last, but that's not true," Johnson contends. "You can still

win and negotiate the best contract, but do it in a very low-key way. You can be strong without being rough." (Yaqub 1995)

I'm blatantly unapologetic about my zeal for good manners. The decreasing levels of civility in our society are cause for alarm. *Managing Your Image Potential* is about much more than outward appearances: It's about being a better, happier, more effective person. Good manners, politeness and kindness are dynamic social levellers and agents of positive change. Be a real revolutionary practising politeness in a world that is rapidly losing its sense of respect.

Maximize your potential:
Good manners are not a sign of weakness.
They can be your greatest strength!

Chapter 12

First Impressions: Making an Entrance

You've arrived at your destination and are about to meet someone for the first time. You pause at the door to straighten your clothing. You've chosen what you're wearing with great care to create a professional image. You discreetly check your hair using the reflection in the window, then take one last look at your shoes. You've prepared what you want to say and are ready to go in.

Standing and Moving with Confidence

Much of the impression you make on others is based on how you look and behave. You can be dressed professionally, impeccably groomed, then undermine your image with poor posture.

Slouching when you're sitting or standing can send messages of defeat, neglect and disinterest. With good posture, your garments hang better, and you look like you're in control. Hold your head erect and practise carrying your ear, shoulder and ankle in alignment. If you're taller than average, take special care to stand tall.

Having poor posture over a long period of time also affects the health of your skeletal system and can lead to chronic back problems.

The speed and confidence with which you move can reflect awareness and self-control. When you enter a room, don't stand meekly just inside the door. Walk a few steps into the room with deliberation, then stand equally balanced on both feet until you're asked to be seated.

Shaking Hands

When you meet someone, especially for the first time, it's customary to offer your hand in greeting. In a business setting, don't hesitate to shake hands, or the person you're meeting will think that you're inexperienced in business protocol.

A handshake will tell you a lot about the person you're meeting, and he or she will also use the opportunity to form opinions about you. I once heard a story about a manager of a local electrical firm who always shakes hands with potential electricians during the interview. If their hands are calloused, the manager takes it as a tangible sign of their work history.

Shaking the hand of someone who holds their arm stiffly is a good example of "keeping someone at arm's length." Be careful—they may not be willing to develop an amicable relationship with you.

Handshake Protocol

Here are some tips on how to shake hands—and how not to.

- Shaking hands in a business setting isn't limited by gender. In the past, shaking hands with women in a social setting wasn't common. Confusion still exists in this area. If you're a woman, extend your hand readily in greeting to avoid any hesitation and awkwardness on the part of the person you're meeting.

• When you do business globally, it's essential that you research the culture of the people you're meeting and be ready to greet them according to their customs. For example, in some countries, physical contact with the opposite sex isn't considered socially acceptable.

• Extend your right hand, even if you're left-handed. If you have a physical disability that prevents you from using your right hand, use your left hand instead. If a person extends their left hand to you for these reasons, don't be embarrassed or draw attention to the irregularity; with a simple twist of your wrist, take hold of their hand and shake hands with your usual enthusiasm.

• Grasp the other person's whole hand firmly, not just their fingers, shake it approximately two or three times, then release it.

• If your hands are cold or clammy, here are some remedies you can try:

> • If you're at a networking session or cocktail party where cold drinks are being served, hold your glass in your left hand. Not only does this keep your right hand closer to body temperature, it avoids having to remove the condensation from your fingers before you shake hands.
>
> • If moist palms are constantly an embarrassment to you, try placing a linen handkerchief, which

you've sprayed with an antiperspirant, into your right pocket. Keep an eye out for an imminent handshake and, before extending your hand, wipe it on the linen cloth. You may need to experiment with the correct amount of antiperspirant to avoid another problem—transferring a sticky residue around the room. Also, use an unscented product.

Avoiding Certain Handshake Styles

When you shake hands with someone, using any of the following styles will give the person the wrong impression.

The Bone Crusher

Some people have no idea how strong their grip is, and there are incidents where muscular handshakes actually break bones. Wait a split second before bearing down to sense the firmness of the other person's grip.

The Cold Fish

Some people make a tentative, limp attempt to shake hands, leaving you feeling as if you've touched a day-old mackerel. You may wonder if the person with such a handshake has any authority or decision-making power. In some cultures, however, gentle, tentative handshakes are the norm.

The Two-Handed Clasp

Cupping another person's hand in both of your hands during a handshake is very inappropriate in a business setting. This sort of handshake is best reserved for close friends and family members.

The Touchy-Feely

Being too affectionate when shaking hands can get you into trouble. Don't put your left hand on the other person's shoulder, and don't put your arm around a person's shoulders—both are too familiar in a business setting. In a social setting, greeting someone like this whom you know well, and when you have their permission to greet them in such a manner, is another matter.

The Arm Wrestle

Handshakes shouldn't be an opportunity for arm wrestling. There are other more effective ways to prove your superiority.

The Upper Hand

Twisting your hand counter-clockwise to achieve an upper-handed position doesn't create a basis for open communication.

Making Eye Contact

Establishing eye contact with acquaintances and business associates is part of making a good impression. In Western culture, averting one's gaze can be a sign of dishonesty or uneasiness. If you have difficulty looking other people in the eye because you're shy, here are some helpful strategies.

- If you're more than three feet away from the person, look at the bridge of their nose. They won't realize that you're doing this.

- When you're closer than three feet, try to detect the colour of the person's eyes. Not only do you need to look the person squarely in the eye, your gaze will rest there for more than a fleeting moment. You can couple this technique with a mnemonic to help you learn the person's name and occupation—for example, "George with blue eyes builds ships that sail the blue sea."

Smiling

You may have heard the saying, "It takes more muscles to frown than it does to smile." In fact, research indicates that the opposite is true. A sincere smile takes effort. When you walk into a new or difficult situation, a smiling face can be one of your best assets. It's easier to meet strangers at a networking session when you smile because it immediately communicates openness, warmth and an invitation to talk. A warm smile will always be remembered.

Maximize your potential:
Make your first impression count!

Chapter 13

Making Introductions

Have you ever been at lunch with a colleague, encountered people whom your associate knows but you don't and you aren't properly introduced to them? Sometimes people are uncertain how to make an introduction, so they avoid it altogether. This is not only rude but, because you can't readily enter into conversation with the third party, it also creates a real communication barrier. Knowing how to introduce friends and colleagues makes social and business situations easier and increases your self-confidence.

Giving an enthusiastic introduction that includes a few words about both people is an excellent conversation starter. For example, "Mr. Brodeur, I want you to meet Kim Bennett, who is a journalism student. Mr. Brodeur is a talented writer." Now Mr. Brodeur and Kim Bennett don't have to resort to small talk but can immediately converse about their mutual interest in writing.

Following the Rules of Introductions

The rules of introductions aren't always clear because there are many factors that need to be considered. One thing is certain: It's better to attempt an introduction than to leave people standing there awkwardly because you fear that you'll make a mistake. If you do commit an obvious social blunder while introducing someone, don't panic! Graceful spontaneity will come to the rescue when good manners prevail. Say you're sorry, then begin the introduction again correctly.

Who Is Introduced to Whom?

When you're faced with introducing someone for the first time, the task becomes a pleasure when you know the basics. The most important rule is set out below.

> Introduce the **younger** or **less important** person
> *to*
> the **older** or **more important** person.

The easiest way to remember this pivotal principle is to *always say the name of the older or more important person first*. Once their name flows from your lips, everything else should fall into place.

The following examples will demonstrate different degrees of formality. When in doubt, use the more formal forms.

"Ms. Black, I'd like you to meet John Smith."
(the older person)   (the younger person)

"Ms. Black, I'd like to present John Smith."
(more formal)

"Ms. Black, may I introduce John Smith?"
(less formal)

"Ms. Black, this is John Smith."
(least formal)

Because John is the less important person, avoid saying: "Ms. Black, I'd like to introduce you to John Smith." By using the preposition *to* twice, John appears more important than Ms. Black. However, you can use this form to correct an introduction if you suddenly realize that you've mistakenly said the less important person's name first. For example: "John Smith, I'd like to introduce you to Ms. Black."

When deciding who is most important, take your cues from:

- the *age* of the people involved
- their *relationship*
- their *position* in business and life
- the *circumstances*

Introducing Family Members

- When introducing a child to an older person, always use the person's title. For example: "Ms. Brownstein, I'd like you to meet my son Jacob."

- Family members are always considered less important than people outside the family, despite rank. For example, elderly Aunt Bertha is considered less important than a younger guest from outside the family. In some families, however, Aunt Bertha may carry such authority that she would never be considered less important than a younger outsider. Common sense and family culture wins out in this situation.

- When you introduce a boyfriend or girlfriend to your parents, your friend is considered more important because he or she is from outside the family.

- When you introduce your spouse to a friend, don't use a formal title, even in formal situations. "Mr. Sanders, I'd like you to meet my spouse, Mr. Fazal" sounds awkward. "Mr. Sanders, I'd like you to meet my spouse, Azis Fazal" is more appropriate.

Including Titles

• If the person you're introducing has a title in addition to their name, include it in the introduction. "Dr. Raj Patel [or Dr. Patel], I'd like to introduce Lisa Dixon, who is one of our generous hospital supporters."

• When you introduce a young person to someone who is considerably older, use the older person's title as a sign of respect. "Mr. Faraklas, I'd like you to meet Jack Winter." It's up to the older person, Mr. Faraklas, to give the younger person permission to use his first name.

Including Last Names

• Always use people's last names; the person includes the whole name. "Mrs. Torres, I want you to meet Kirsten" isn't enough. If you don't recall Kirsten's last name, try to find out before you begin the introduction.

When Age and Rank Collide

• When rank and age collide, let common sense be your guide. Let's say that John Tse is an important judge, but he's quite a bit younger than Mr. McPhail. It would be courteous to introduce Judge Tse to Mr. McPhail. "Mr. McPhail, may I introduce Judge Tse?"

Clarifying Relationships

• If you're introducing a couple with different last names, it can be helpful to make their relationship clear. "I'd like you to meet Dianne Parke and her husband, David Jones."

• When you introduce the child of a woman who goes by her maiden name, include the child's family name. Using the example of the couple above, if David Jones was introducing his daughter to Ms. Johnson, he'd say: "Ms. Johnson, I'd like you to meet my daughter, Sarah Parke."

• When introducing a couple living together, it can be helpful to make their relationship clear. "I'd like you to meet Chris Ranft and his companion, Larry Fine." Or: "I'd like you to meet Pam Sager and her partner, Ajit John."

Don't Repeat Names

• When you make an introduction, don't repeat the names of the people, as shown in this example: "Mr. Wong . . . Mr. Ducharme. Mr. Ducharme . . . Mr Wong." Only say their names again if you want to give more information about them: "Mr. Wong, I'd like you to meet Mr. Ducharme. Mr. Ducharme competed in the Olympics last year. Mr. Wong hopes to take part in the next winter games."

Don't Use "My Friend"

• Be careful not to use the words "my friend" when introducing someone because it sounds like the other person isn't a friend. Instead, you can say: "Stephanie Williams, I'd like you to meet my neighbour, Jennifer Ng. Stephanie and I attended the same high school."

Handling Gender

• In business today, gender is no longer an issue in introductions, whereas in social situations, a man is always introduced to a woman. When you introduce someone in a business setting, make their position in the company clear to avoid the embarrassment of a manager being mistaken for an administrative assistant or vice versa.

Responding to an Introduction

• When someone is introduced to you, some good responses are: "How do you do?" or "It's nice to meet you."

• Don't use unnatural responses such as: "Charmed!" "Delighted!" or "Pleased to make your acquaintance."

• "I've heard a lot about you" has also become a cliché. Usually it prompts the reply, "I hope it was good." A more meaningful comment, and one that easily leads to conversation, is: "I've heard that you're an avid golfer." (Substitute any other appropriate interest.)

Rising When You're Being Introduced

In most social situations, it's considered polite that when a woman enters the room for the first time, the men rise and stay standing until the woman is seated, leaves the room or says, "Please take your seats."

When a client, man or woman, enters your office, it's polite to rise, offer them a chair, then sit down once they've been seated. When they're ready to leave, the procedure is similar: Rise and escort them to the door.

Forgetting Names

Embarrassing situations occur when you're unable to recall names. As I mentioned earlier, if you're with a friend and you encounter another person you've previously met, it's polite to make introductions. If you've forgotten the person's name, simply make an apology and ask to be reminded of it. For example, "Your face is so familiar, but I'm sorry—I've forgotten your name. Would you please refresh my memory?" The person will usually tell you their name, and you can then make the introduction.

When you're alone and you meet someone you've met before, but you can't recall their name, simply say: "Hello. I know we've met before. Would you please remind me of your name and/or the circumstances?" It's important to do this immediately because you may find yourself encountering a third person and then you won't be able to make introductions.

Maximize your potential:
Practise making introductions!

Chapter 14

Improving Your Business Image

Being a Responsible Person

Your reputation as a reliable person is essential to your success in both your personal and your professional life. Keeping appointments and promises are the backbone of good business relationships. Never promise what you can't deliver. If you tell your clients one thing and do another, you'll soon lose credibility, and without credibility, you cannot build trust.

There should be no surprises for your clients regarding your product, service, invoice or delivery. Follow up clients' affairs carefully, and when you call them, keep current information regarding their accounts or contracts nearby. If you need to change a delivery date, give clients as much advanced warning as possible. If you're using associates or subcontractors to complete the work, you're answerable for their actions; make sure they understand their responsibilities and keep things under control.

Being Reliable by Managing Your Time

Time management affects many details of your business life, and ultimately, your image. Being late causes serious damage to your professional stature. Chronic lateness dramatically influences the way you and your business are perceived by existing and potential customers. Are you and your staff reliable in the eyes of your clients?

Learn to budget your time so that you can provide your service effectively and efficiently. Prioritize your commitments daily and refer to them often throughout your working day. Schedule time to develop both short-term and long-term goals, set priorities, prepare for business meetings, follow up clients, return telephone calls and complete correspondence. To avoid a possible crisis, ensure that the timelines you've set for yourself are realistic.

If you need to travel to a meeting, allocate an appropriate amount of time to get there on schedule. Build in time buffers for unexpected interruptions. And always allocate time for yourself. Although taking a short break in the middle of a frenzied business day may feel like wasted time, it will actually make you more productive in the long run.

Handling Interruptions

Be prepared for interruptions, and discipline yourself to quickly refocus your energies once a problem is resolved. If someone arrives unannounced at your office and you have a deadline to meet, politely inform them of the fact and ask them to return at a scheduled time.

If the person is a customer, you must exercise care in handling this interruption. Emergency situations affecting clients must be dealt with quickly. But if it's not urgent, consider saying that because you appreciate them, you insist on giving them your undivided attention and would like to schedule an appointment with them. Set this appointment immediately and for a time within the next 24 hours. To show the client further consideration, suggest that you'll travel to their location for the meeting.

Respecting Everyone

Treat everyone with respect, whatever their status or your corporate agenda. With an increasingly aging population, demographics experts predict that there will soon be a shortage of experienced, knowledgeable personnel. The workforce will be enriched with seniors who've chosen not to retire. This demographic reality will affect relationships on the job, and managers may have workers with 30 or 40 years' more experience reporting to them. Displaying leadership, while still respecting these people's knowledge, will create a healthy and productive work environment.

Here are a number of other guidelines to follow to show respect.

- If it's necessary to reprimand someone, never do it in front of others. Take the person aside in a private area before speaking with them.

- Defend colleagues when they've been wronged. Although it's easier to remain silent, your interaction will be greatly appreciated and will build goodwill within the company.

- In a formal business setting, show deference to senior people by not speaking to them on a first-name basis unless they've permitted you to do so. There is nothing more annoying than being addressed by a stranger in an overly familiar manner. Respect must be earned.

- Never gossip or engage in destructive criticism behind colleagues' backs; gossip can cause the downfall of both the victim and the perpetrator. Don't waste company time in idle conversation. Time is money.

- Learn how to make open-ended conversation and how to listen carefully. When you talk with a client or colleague, clear your mind and concentrate on what he or she is saying. This attitude not only shows the person respect but also ensures that fewer misunderstandings occur. Ask intelligent questions and listen to colleagues' questions. When you deal with a complaint or problem, establish a middle ground quickly; this shows others that you can be fair and objective.

- Respect other peoples' territory and learn to avoid interrupting your colleagues.

  - If you need to see someone, call ahead to find out if they're free.

  - If their office door is closed, don't barge in, expecting them to drop everything for you. Making a telephone call to arrange for an appropriate time is not only polite but will also guarantee their full attention.

- If your colleague maintains an open door policy, always knock before entering to make your presence known and avoid startling them.

- Respecting territory is particularly important in an open-office concept. When no physical barrier exists between you and your colleagues, don't interrupt them without good cause.

- Respect also extends to possessions. When you borrow an item from a colleague, tell them when you expect to return it and do so promptly. Treat company property with care.

Creating Loyalty Inside and Outside the Company

Management often overlooks the benefits that a company can derive from a positive image. Image alone can be the factor that makes customers decide whether to do business with your company. The better your company's image, the more money it'll make, and the more it can afford to pay its staff.

A disgruntled employee can create a negative, destructive atmosphere that is always damaging to productivity. If the person exhibits this attitude outside the company, it will inevitably affect your business. If existing or potential clients hear you complaining about the company you work for, they'll begin to doubt the quality of your company's product or service. If you persist, they'll eventually take their business to a competitor. Remember the saying: "Never bite the hand that feeds you." If you differ with company policy, use constructive ways to bring about positive change; if this strategy doesn't work, examine your options for employment elsewhere.

Employers can also create loyalty within their company by demonstrating a positive and supportive attitude towards their employees at all times. If managers are cordial to their employees in view of clients, but unpleasant behind the scenes, they'll ultimately affect their company's success. Constructive criticism is far more productive than glaring disapproval.

Managing Effectively

There are a number of things you can do to manage staff effectively.

- Make sure that your employees have a proper, safe work environment.

- Never expect an employee to follow a rule you don't follow yourself. The golden rule really works in all walks of life.

- Make newcomers welcome.

- Help those on the ladder below you and thank them for their support.

- Show compassion to an employee who's received bad news.

- Encourage those who are discouraged.

- Don't work during an office party.

Erring on the Side of Generosity

It's wiser and more effective for your image to err on the side of generosity in business situations. Consider developing a personal philosophy as a guide for your life. The following quote from George Eliot on the purpose of life is a good example: "What are we here for, if not to make the world less difficult for each other?" A genuine and generous spirit will open many doors of opportunity.

- Acknowledge favours with a note of thanks or a phone call.

- Recognize a special promotion, an award or an outstanding job.

- Take time to congratulate a colleague or business associate in writing. This has a greater impact than a verbal message.

- Give credit where credit is due.

- Don't accept praise for something you haven't done.

- Don't hoard information; instead, keep people informed of business developments. Ultimately, it's more productive.

- Always reciprocate invitations for a business lunch.

Giving and Receiving Gifts

It's common to receive gifts from suppliers or to give gifts to clients in acknowledgement for business received from them. However, gifts can be construed as bribery. As a result, some companies have a "no gift" policy, or they ask suppliers to direct the funds that would have been used to purchase gifts to a charity. It's important for managers to make this company policy clear to their employees before an awkward situation arises and a gift must be returned.

If you're doing business in the global marketplace, research the customs of the countries with which you're working because gifts may be part of their business culture. To avoid embarrassment, learn which gifts aren't appropriate. For example, never give white flowers to a Japanese person—they're associated with death. Also in Japan, where giving gifts in a business setting is common, a gift can be quite simple, but the ceremony of giving it is quite elaborate.

Replying to Invitations

Many people today tend to ignore the R.S.V.P. on invitations. *R.S.V.P.*

is an acronym for the French phrase, *Répondez s'il vous plaît* (Please reply).

You wouldn't think of showing up at a wedding reception without first informing the bride; the same applies to a business event. Check the invitation closely to see if there is an R.S.V.P. and a date, then call the sender before that date to say whether you can attend. Your host will appreciate an early reply. (For more guidance on social practices that influence your personal life, consult one of the many detailed etiquette handbooks in your library or bookstore.)

Sending Notes of Thanks

In the hectic pace of life, saying "thank you" has almost become a dying art. Acknowledging staff and colleagues for a job well done is an effective way to encourage excellence. A note of thanks sent within a reasonable amount of time for a gift you've received, a special dinner, a testimonial, a business referral, etc. will enhance your image and your business relationships.

A handwritten note is more meaningful than a typed letter and much more effective than an e-mail message, which is easy to dash off and can come across as cold and impersonal. The format you use will depend on the context and the person you're writing. For example, if you were writing a person in authority to thank them for a dinner they gave in your honour, e-mail wouldn't suffice; you'd need to send a formal letter. On the other hand, an e-mail message would be acceptable to thank a close colleague for a referral they gave you. Sending handwritten thank-you notes to your clients will definitely impress them. After a job interview, you can increase your chances of being hired by about 30 per cent by sending your potential employer a typed (and error-free) letter of thanks.

Practising E-Mail Etiquette

Unless you use video-conferencing facilities when you communicate electronically, you cannot provide visual or audio clues to help the other person interpret your message. You can't influence the reader using facial expressions, posture, hand movements or the tone and speed of your voice. All you have is the written word on the screen, so choose your words carefully, and remember that although e-mail is impersonal, you're communicating with real people.

The following are just a few guidelines to help you maintain your professionalism in cyberspace. You'll find more information on the Internet.

- Keep the same standards that you use when you're face to face with the person. The anonymity of electronic communication is no excuse for rudeness.

- Keep your messages brief, but don't be cryptic. Brevity may save bandwidth and time, but it doesn't foster good business relationships.

- Don't forget to give your name; signing with your initials can be confusing.

- Even if your company encourages lowercase for internal memos, use correct spelling, punctuation and grammar when you send messages outside the company.

- At work, keep your messages related to business. Many companies are now monitoring e-mail; being caught misusing the system for personal messages could be your undoing.

- Don't send your message several times in a row to get the receiver's attention. Instead, mark it Urgent. Don't overuse this technique because like the boy who cried wolf, you may be ignored when you really need an answer.

- USING ALL CAPITAL LETTERS IS EQUAL TO SHOUTING. Keep your tone of voice professional.

- Remember that unless your e-mail software uses encryption, assume that Internet communication isn't secure. Don't write anything that you wouldn't write on a postcard.

- Don't send chain letters.

- If you're forwarding a message, don't change the wording. If the e-mail was personal or confidential, ask the sender's permission to forward it.

- If you're replying to an e-mail, don't click the Reply button and begin typing. To make your message shorter, easier to read and to save time, quote only the necessary lines to put your reply into context.

- Use a subject line that refers to the subject matter. Continue to use this line on subsequent messages that relate to the topic being discussed.

- Don't send abusive messages.

- Make sure that you accurately address your mail.

- Once you've written a message, store it in your Outbox while you go on to the next message. A few moments of reflection may cause you to change the content slightly. Once you click the Send button, you can't take the message back. If you're addressing a particularly difficult situation that isn't pressing, you may want to wait 24 hours and review your words before sending the message.

- Although we expect a message to arrive instantly at its destination, there are many reasons for delays—different time zones, a lot of traffic on the lines, etc. Be patient.

- Keep your signature to three or four lines.

- E-mail tends to encourage informality. If you're doing business globally, especially in Asia, use a more formal approach and include the person's title—for example, "Dr. Cheung." When in doubt, start more formally. If the person replies using your first name, do likewise.

- In a business context, eliminate smileys such as (:-) and ;-).

- Avoid sending unsolicited e-mail. It will be considered junk e-mail.

Maximize your potential:
Improve your business image by following the three Rs: Responsibility, reliability and respect!

Chapter 15

Meeting Manners

In a meeting, you reveal a lot about yourself and your potential. It's the perfect arena for demonstrating your leadership skills, ability to interact with others, communication savvy and presentation ability. It's also an environment where others can discover whether you're on top of your responsibilities and can be trusted with further matters.

Call a meeting only when you have a clear purpose. There is nothing more frustrating than to be in a meeting that has no direction. If you don't know the purpose of the meeting, how can you expect the participants to contribute effectively? Most people dislike attending meetings because they're often disorganized, too little gets accomplished and they feel like their time has been wasted.

Time is often equated to money. When you bring people from a distance to a central location for a meeting, not only do you have to consider the expense of their transportation, meals, accommodation and room rental, but you must also consider the costs associated with allocating professional time to a meeting. Weigh these financial expenses against what you hope to accomplish. Ask yourself whether the purpose of your meeting could be achieved by a teleconference, e-mail or virtual discussion.

Once you've decided that face-to-face interaction is the best solution, the following guidelines will help you manage your meeting effectively.

Timing Considerations

Effective meetings make the best use of everyone's time.

- Try to avoid calling a meeting at the end of a day or on the day before a long weekend. People won't be as co-operative and creative when they're tired or preoccupied.

- Inform participants well in advance so that they can block off the time. This could mean giving as much as four to six weeks' notice.

- Indicate the approximate length of the meeting.

- Start the meeting on time, even if all the participants haven't arrived. This is respectful of those who were prompt.

Participant Involvement

The participants you invite also contribute to productive meetings.

- Invite only those who are directly involved. When you're trying to make decisions, a smaller group is more effective than a large one.

- Invite participants who are open-minded and not afraid

to express their ideas. They'll add more to a meeting than those who always agree with the status quo.

The Agenda

Making up a concise agenda ensures that meetings are only as long as they need to be.

- Prepare a detailed agenda stating the purpose of the meeting, the location, a list of items to be discussed, time allocations and the person(s) responsible for each area.

- Distribute the agenda well in advance and have extra copies at the meeting.

- Include with the agenda the minutes of the last meeting and any information that participants need to study ahead of time.

Seating

The seating arrangement can follow a particular protocol and have its own purpose.

- Wait to be seated or take the seat farthest away from the Chair.

- At a rectangular table, the Chair usually sits at one end, and senior management and honoured guests sit on either side.

- If delegates from other countries attend, seat them on the long side of the table facing the door so that they can see anyone entering the room. Sit your group opposite them. The most senior people would sit in the centre of each group.

- If you sit in the seat opposite the Chair, you'll be directly in their line of vision, so stay alert! This is a good seat if you want the Chair's attention.

- If you want to mitigate a confrontation, avoid sitting directly opposite the person in question. This avoids direct eye contact and possible conflict.

The Role of the Chair

Being an effective Chair ensures that meetings run smoothly and show off your leadership skills.

- Ensure that the essential people are there.

- Welcome participants and introduce those who don't know each other.

- Show people to their seats.

- Lay down the ground rules and conduct the meeting according to the agenda.

- If you want someone to record the proceedings and to keep the meeting on track, assign a Recorder, Timekeeper and Agenda Monitor.

- Encourage everyone to participate.

- If the meetings occur regularly, set a date for the next meeting.

- Thank participants and supportive administrative staff, and give a special thanks to those who made presentations.

- Ensure that the Recorder distributes the minutes within

48 hours after the meeting with notes on who is responsible for follow-up actions.

The Role of the Participant

Being a co-operative participant shows that you're a team player.

- Arrive on time with your homework done (read the agenda, bring any materials, comments and so on).

- Introduce yourself to those you don't know.

- Wait for the Chair to seat you.

- Turn off your cellphone and make calls during breaks.

- Behave in a professional way: Sit upright, appear alert, don't play with pens and so on.

- Listen to what is being said and let your body language reflect your attention.

- Don't carry on private conversations or make comments when someone else is speaking.

- Don't be afraid to ask intelligent and clarifying questions.

- Don't interrupt or attempt to hijack the meeting to discuss your pet project. Make concise comments relevant to the discussion at the appropriate time.

- If you need to leave the meeting, excuse yourself politely and re-enter quietly.

- Thank the Chair before you leave.

Maximizing Your Potential

You can use meetings to reveal your communication savvy.

- If you have an option about where to sit, choose a spot where you'll be noticed by the decision makers.

- Speaking up early in the meeting will assert your presence. Only do this if you're sure of the topic being discussed and have something valuable to add; otherwise, remain silent until you can contribute effectively.

- If you're not being listened to, ask for a response to what you've said: "Before we discuss fundraising, I'd like to hear the group's response to what I've said."

- When you propose a new idea or solution, use tact *but don't undermine yourself.* "I don't know if this will work" isn't as effective as "There is a possible solution here. Let's try ..."

- Avoid other self-deprecating words or phrases such as "This may be dumb ..." or "This is just a ..."

- Control your voice and avoid finishing your sentences with an upward inflection that makes you sound like you're asking a question instead of making a statement. (For more detail, refer to the chapter on verbal communication.)

Making a Presentation

Effective presentations show off your polished professional image.

- Know why you're making a presentation. What is the purpose? Is there a business decision to be made? Are you training? If you're not clear, ask!

- Find out how the meeting room will be set up for you so you can prepare your presentation for the best physical impact. All participants must be able to see.

- If you're entering a meeting in progress, suggest to the Chair that the participants take a short break while you set up so that you'll have their full attention when you begin your talk.

- Keep track of the time and stay within the limits you've been given.

Teleconferences

Participating in meetings conducted over the telephone requires a unique set of meeting manners.

- When you join the call, announce yourself.

- Don't create background noises by rustling paper, typing on a keyboard close to the receiver, etc.

- Once most people are on the line, the Chair will verify who is present and call the meeting to order.

- The Chair will follow the agenda closely, and only one person should talk at a time. Wait until your turn and speak only when you're addressed by the Chair unless general comments are requested. If you have an opportunity to express your opinion, state your name before you speak. Not everyone will know you by your voice.

- Keep your discussion focused on the agenda items and be mindful of the scheduled time.

- At the end of the call, the Chair will summarize, close and thank the participants.

Handling Meeting Challenges

There will always be challenges in meetings that try the patience of the participants. To maintain your professional stance, it's important to handle these situations with tact so that no one loses face and the meeting isn't disrupted.

Late Arrivals

When someone arrives late, don't repeat the material that has already been covered. This not only wastes time but also penalizes those who were there on time. At a break or after the meeting, the latecomer can speak to the Recorder to see what was missed. If the latecomer is habitually tardy, the Chair should address the problem with the person privately after the meeting.

Reluctant Participants

Some people are hesitant to speak at meetings and require some encouragement from the Chair. Instead of saying: "You haven't said anything during the whole meeting," you can try: "I know you've worked on this project, and we'd value your opinion on this matter." If the person doesn't have a reply, suggest that you return for ideas later. This will give time for a thoughtful response.

Constant Commentators

There are people who feel it necessary to monopolize the conversation and comment on each agenda item. This not only slows the progress of the meeting, but it hinders those who are shy or reluctant to speak up. Constant commentators must be respected but also controlled. Thank them for their contribution and then ask to hear from others. If you're aware of the problem beforehand, you can outline at the beginning of the meeting how you want participants to give feedback. You can also ask that comments be held until all the topics have been presented. Sometimes breaking the participants into groups and having them work as a team to report their thoughts is also effective.

Private Conversations

People who talk to their neighbours during a meeting not only disrupt those around them but are also being plainly impolite. So as not to confront them with equal rudeness, tactfully invite the person to share with the whole group. This may draw the person into the meeting. If the talking persists, being silent until the talking stops also speaks volumes.

Co-opters

Some participants will want to lead the discussion away from the planned agenda to their pet projects. The Chair or Agenda Monitor can place such items in the "Issue Bin" until the end of the meeting, when "Other Business" is covered, time permitting.

Put-Downs

There will always be someone who thinks that his or her idea is the only idea worth considering. To handle this situation, the Chair can remind the whole group that personal experiences may differ and that therefore all views are valid, even if they're unusual or unpopular. Solutions will vary according to circumstances, and understanding what others experience or perceive will make everyone more effective.

Maximize your potential:
Ensure effective, productive meetings!

Chapter 16

Telephone Manners

Telephone manners are another important aspect of your business image. When you speak on the telephone, cultivate good telephone manners and be consistent in how you use them.

Answering the Telephone

The way you answer the telephone sets the mood for the conversation that follows. The following points will help you make a prime impression.

• Always smile when you answer the telephone, even if you don't feel like it. You'll sound more approachable and friendly.

• You don't want to sound like your voice is contrived; in times of stress, you won't be able to keep it up. A natural, well-modulated, friendly voice is best. A harsh tone isn't welcoming; and a lack of enthusiasm doesn't inspire callers to continue the conversation.

- If you're feeling rushed, take a deep breath before you answer the telephone.

- "Hello" is best. "Yes?" is abrupt. "Good morning, John Brown speaking" is appropriate in a business setting, while "Mr. Brown" would be used in a formal office setting.

- When you take a call for someone else, inform the caller that you're putting them on hold. If the telephone doesn't have a Hold feature, place your hand over the mouthpiece before locating the recipient of the call.

- Be careful not to use slang such as "Yeah, hang on" or "No problem." If you do this without thinking, try to visualize the caller standing in front of you as you speak.

- If the person receiving the call isn't readily available, ask the caller if they'd like to leave a message. Take down enough information: full name, telephone number, company, date and time of the call and, if possible, the reason for the call.

- Don't mumble or speak too loudly. When you speak loudly, you can interrupt your co-workers.

- Have patience with those who need more time to explain the purpose of their call. In our fast-paced society, it's easy to be abrupt in an attempt to move the conversation along.

- Don't answer the telephone when a guest or customer is present. Take a message or let the call go to voice mail, then return the call.

- Mute the ring on the telephone before you begin a meeting.

- If you've initiated a call and have a feature on your telephone that beeps when another call comes in, don't interrupt your conversation abruptly to see who it is; the person you're talking to will feel unimportant. (In cases where you know the person well, you may ask permission to answer the call. If you answer the call, take a brief message, then tell the caller that you'll call them right back.)

Making Calls

It's equally important to be courteous and polite when you make a call. Your colleague could answer the phone themselves, or they could ask his or her administrative assistant what their impression is of you.

• Let the telephone ring six to ten times. Nothing is more annoying than to leave a task to answer the telephone only to have the caller hang up after three rings.

• It's courteous to say your name before asking for the person you're calling. For example, "Hello, this is Yuta Smardenka calling. I'd like to speak with John Evans." Adding your company name helps avoid the embarrassment of not being remembered.

• If you telephone someone and the line becomes disconnected, the onus is on you to call the person back.

• If you call the wrong number, it's polite to say, "I'm sorry to have disturbed you" before you hang up and try again.

Returning Calls

In our hectic business lives, the telephone messages can easily mount up. You'll be recognized as a true professional simply by returning your telephone calls promptly.

- Check your messages at least three times a day and return telephone calls before the end of the business day, even to say that you don't yet have an answer. If it's not possible to get back to the person on the same day, do so within 24 hours. It's damaging to your professional image to wait longer than a day. The person may incorrectly assume that you think they're not important and take their business elsewhere.

- Always return telephone calls, even if you suspect that you're not interested in the product or service that the caller is offering. After listening to the person, politely state your opinion.

Voice Mail and Message Services

Voice mail, answering machines and message services increase efficiency. Here are a few tips to maximize your time and potential.

- With the increase in small businesses that operate at all hours, it's more practical to leave a message than to continuously call until you find the person in their office.

- When you leave a message, give your full name, company, telephone number and reason for calling. In this way, if the person you're calling encounters your voice mail when they return your call, they can leave you a detailed message. It may help alleviate telephone tag. It also allows the person to bring the necessary information to the telephone instead of having to call back a second time.

- When you leave your telephone number in your message, speak slowly and clearly. Say it at the beginning of the message and repeat it at the end. This allows the person to check your number without having to replay the message.

• When you create your outgoing message that the caller hears, make sure that it's professional. The sound of throbbing music in the background, or ice tinkling in a glass, doesn't give the appropriate impression.

Home-Based Businesses

Home-based businesses are often judged to be less professional than those established outside the home. To alleviate such an impression, here are a few tips.

• If you operate a business from your home, answer the telephone just as you would as if you had a business established somewhere else.

• Install a separate business telephone line, or take advantage of a service that identifies whether the call is personal or business in nature.

• Everyone who answers the telephone in your house should be taught how to properly handle calls. A very young child answering your business telephone might not be helpful to a caller.

Using Cellular Telephones and Pagers

Cellular telephones and pagers have become a common and necessary part of business communication. However, they can become a nuisance if they're not handled properly. Here are some guidelines on using them.

- Don't allow the convenience that these devices provide to become an excuse for rude interruptions. If you're expecting an important call that you can't miss, inform the person you're with that you may have to take a call. When it comes, the interruption won't seem as rude.

- If you're in a public place such as a theatre, restaurant, lecture hall or place of worship, cellular telephones and pagers are out of place unless you can be notified of a call using a silent vibration. In this case, quietly excuse yourself and take the call away from the others present.

Avoiding Pitfalls

When you're talking on the telephone, you don't see the other person. It's easy to create distractions that can become barriers to communication. Here are some pitfalls to avoid.

- Don't talk to another person in the room while you're on the telephone.

- Take your calls away from annoying background noise caused by a printer, photocopier, entertainment system, etc.

- Don't eat, chew gum, smoke or drink while you're talking on the telephone.

- Don't rustle papers, work on your computer or sound distracted when you're on the telephone. The person you're speaking to will know that you're not being attentive.

- Don't tap your fingers impatiently or sigh as you wait for the caller to finish a sentence. The caller can easily detect these signs of impatience.

- Don't sneeze, breath heavily or cough directly into the mouthpiece.

Telephone Interviews

Many companies use the telephone to shorten a long list of job applicants or interview candidates who live a considerable distance away. If you find yourself in the position of being interviewed on the telephone, be mindful that your energy level is just as important as your answers. You'll sound more enthusiastic if you stand and move about while you're talking. At all costs, avoid the pitfalls listed above so that you'll make a great first impression.

Maximize your potential:
Communicate using good telephone manners!

Chapter 17

Conversational Manners

Conversation is becoming a dying art. In a social context, people are spending more time on their own, watching television and surfing the Internet. Families seldom gather around a dining table to talk during and after a meal.

In business, the work day is crowded with decisions that need to be made quickly, with no time left to chat. With all this activity, there is little opportunity to develop the conversational manners that will reflect positively on your ability to conduct yourself appropriately in all circumstances.

Showing Courtesy

One of the most important aspects of good communication is being courteous. Interrupting, talking too much—especially about controversial subjects—and talking down to someone show that you're self-centred or simply nervous. Good listening skills will always help you show courtesy during the most difficult conversations.

Discussing Controversial Subjects

Religion, politics and morality can be considered controversial subjects that require much knowledge and tact to escape heated arguments. It's best to avoid these subjects altogether. If you're discussing something controversial, listen to the other side, then state your opinions with care so as not to appear like a know-it-all with a hardened point of view.

Interrupting

It's rude to break into a conversation and interrupt the speaker. Remain silent and wait for an opportunity to state your opinion. When you're interrupted, wait for a few seconds and then return to the point you were making. Avoid the tendency to finish other people's sentences.

Talking Too Much

It's difficult to stop a person from talking too much, especially when they don't know they're doing it. Sometimes your complete silence will help the person realize that they've taken over, but you mustn't appear rude. You can wait for a strategic moment, when an exchange of new ideas might alter the one-sided conversation. If you become aware that you've been monopolizing the conversation, apologize and ask the other person an open-ended question.

Talking above or down to Someone

Be sensitive to the people you're speaking to. Make a sincere effort to converse in a manner that includes others by avoiding any tendency to patronize or alienate them.

Telling Stories Repeatedly

If someone tells stories repeatedly, after the second time, inform the person that you've heard the story before by saying something like: "Oh, I recall that story. It certainly left an impression on you." Always be positive with your comments and then quickly change the subject.

If you're a storyteller, you can be in danger of repeating stories more than once. When in doubt, ask the person you're with if you've shared it with them before, and if you have, change the subject.

Being a Good Listener

When you listen attentively, you give the other person the impression that their opinions are important. Learn how to really hear what the person is saying. Do you give the impression that you're paying attention, while in reality, you're waiting to break into the conversation or looking for an opportunity to change the subject?

Practising Plain Courtesy

Give plain courtesy precedence over political correctness. Courtesy will far outlast the changes that occur in social awareness. Celebrate and support ethnic and cultural diversity; this is the real world we live in. Successful businesses are expanding across the globe. Don't make fun of people who have regional accents or expressions.

Don't take part in ethnic jokes. If you're alone with a person who tells such jokes, tell them that they make you uncomfortable. If you're in a group, walk away without commenting.

If you need to refer to someone's cultural background, learn what is appropriate because changes occur over time. For example:

- *African-Canadians*, *African-Americans* and *Blacks* have replaced *Negroes*.

- *Asian* is acceptable; *Oriental* isn't.

- People who have a disability aren't *disabled*. They're people *with* a physical or developmental disability.

In all these cases, it's best not to segregate people into categories based on race, gender or physical abilities but to refer to them as persons on an equal footing.

Admitting You're Wrong and Apologizing

Don't be afraid to admit that you're wrong—it can only help your character. It's important to put your feelings aside and make an apology because unresolved conflicts result in bitterness that destroys friendships and business relationships. If it doesn't make light of the apology, use humour. "I'm sorry" isn't enough for an apology: Give a reason. For example: "I'm sorry I'm late. I had car trouble and couldn't call you."

Handling Compliments

We usually feel self-conscious when someone pays us a compliment. Instead of being embarrassed, learn to handle the situation with politeness and ease.

Acknowledging a Compliment

Don't sound embarrassed or try to pass a compliment off as false. Reply with enthusiasm: "Thank you. I appreciate your positive comments" or "It was definitely one of my better presentations" or "Thank you, I'm glad that you found it interesting."

Paying a Compliment

Everyone enjoys a compliment, but make sure that you're sincere because insincerity always has a way of showing. Don't gush or overstate the compliment. Insecure people find it hard to praise others; secure people are generous with their praise.

Passing on a Compliment

A second-hand compliment carries more weight than a direct one. For example: "Nancy told me of your recent performance award. Congratulations!" Passing on a compliment demonstrates your generous spirit.

Avoiding Pitfalls

As soon as you've said something inappropriate, you want to put something large into your mouth to stop you from doing it again—hence the old saying, "I've put my foot in my mouth." Sometimes you're not aware that you've upset someone, but if you see a sudden change in their face or body language, check for one of these pitfalls.

Personal Questions

Your natural curiosity will often impede communication. There are many personal questions that can be offensive to others. Avoid the following topics at all costs:

- someone's age
- whether someone has had cosmetic surgery
- why someone isn't married
- why a couple doesn't have children

- what someone does for a living (the person may be unemployed or underemployed; if they don't do something they think is exciting, they may feel inferior telling you this)
- the reason for someone's physical problem (limp, lack of limb, bruises, scars, bandages, etc.)
- how much money someone earns
- whether someone has lost or gained weight
- someone's sexual orientation

Unanswered Questions

If you ask where a person purchased a garment that you admire and they say, "I can't remember," don't push the issue. The person may not want to answer the question and would be embarrassed if you asked a second time. Similarly, it's considered bad manners to ask how much something costs (unless the person being questioned is a close friend and you know they won't mind). If you enjoy a friend's culinary delight and ask for the recipe but it isn't offered to you, don't ask for it again. Serious cooks can be quite secretive.

Bragging and Name Dropping

Bragging doesn't elevate your reputation; it shows that you're self-centred. Ignore someone who is bragging, and they'll usually stop. Mentioning the name of a prominent person you know is acceptable, but if it develops into a habit, it becomes name-dropping, a particularly irritating form of bragging.

If someone is always dropping names, ask a few detailed questions about the prominent person. If they don't know the person well and can't answer the questions, they'll probably not mention their name again.

Using Too Many Superlatives

When you're trying to make a very valid point about yourself, your product or your service, often in the face of an objection or criticism, you may get lost in your enthusiasm. In trying to promote your position, you can in fact undermine it by overstating your case. Avoid using too many superlatives. If you use a lot of adjectives and adverbs, especially when you're on the defensive, your message may be rejected as insincere. It's best to present your position with confidence, enthusiasm and reasonableness rather than with too much verbiage and inappropriate emphasis.

Obscene Jokes and Swearing

Don't tell obscene jokes to impress or entertain people; it'll make you seem juvenile. If you're on the receiving end, a good reply is: "I don't respond well to that kind of humour." Try to steer the conversation in a more positive direction.

Profanity is not powerful. Swearing does nothing to raise your image. Rise above those who use swear words by not using them yourself.

Gossip

Don't become entangled in the grapevine. Gossiping doesn't enhance your image, and it never respects confidentiality. Refusing to participate in gossip can cause positive change in your relationships and surroundings.

Giving Unsolicited Advice

It's difficult, and often inappropriate, to give advice when you're not asked for it. People will understandably resent it. If you think that giving your advice will save someone's job or marriage, it may be worth the risk, but your advice must be supported with facts and be non-judgmental. Be aware that the person may still reject your well-meaning words.

Embarrassing Situations

If you notice that a friend has their fly open, a button undone, or spinach in their teeth, try to tell them without drawing more attention to it. If you don't know the person, ask one of their friends who's present to tell them.

Maximize your potential:
Cultivate good conversational manners!

Chapter 18

Verbal Communication

Most people don't realize that 38 per cent of the first impression they make on others comes from their voice (Mehrabian 1981, 76). Unless a person's career involves a lot of talking, such as in politics or the media, most people pay little attention to how they speak. Thus, when they focus on their image, they often overlook their voice. It's important that what you say is consistent with how you say it.

Tempo

The *tempo,* or speed at which you talk affects your listener. People who speak with a faster tempo are more persuasive than people who speak slowly. For example, people who speak about 190 words per minute are perceived as being more trustworthy and enthusiastic. It's often effective to match the tempo of your voice with that of the person with whom you're speaking.

Many people are uncomfortable with silence, so they completely fill the air with their words. If you do this, you lessen your effectiveness because your audience can't digest what you're saying while you're talking. Pauses are powerful; not only do they help your listener comprehend what you're saying, but you can also use them to emphasize your most important points.

Tone

Tone refers to whether you have a high or low voice. A high, squeaky voice can definitely affect your image potential. In politics, women have more difficulty establishing their credibility because their voices are generally lighter and higher in tone. A voice with a lower tone automatically projects more authority. If your voice is high, practise lowering it one-half octave by relaxing the muscles in your throat and learning to breathe from your diaphragm.

Inflection

Many women, and some men, end their sentences on an upward inflection, as if they're asking a question rather than making a statement. This immediately erodes a strong image. Practise saying the following sentences to a friend and ask them to listen for any upward inflection so that you can correct this tendency:

- I realize the importance of this contract; however, without additional resources, I'll be unable to meet the deadline.
- I wish you every success in your new job.
- This training program is just as important to me as it is to the company.
- Jack, I'm sorry. You'll be unable to take your vacation in July.
- Because you've had difficulty meeting agreed-on goals and objectives, I find it necessary to terminate your employment.

- Sales have increased 30 per cent since I joined the team, so I'd like a comparable increase in my salary.
- It was my mistake. I should have been aware of the problem.
- I respect your opinion, but I want the job done according to my plan.
- Because I gave you an extension on the deadline and the work is still not done, I want to know why you haven't completed it.
- I know I can do it.

Tips for a Healthy Voice

Straining your vocal chords to be heard above a noisy environment can cause permanent damage. Don't speak so loudly that your voice cracks. If necessary, use non-vocal strategies to make your point.

Many professional speakers warm up their voices before an engagement by singing a favourite song several times. Learn to support your voice with proper breathing techniques. Even if you don't aspire to a musical career, it would be helpful to arrange for a few coaching sessions with a voice teacher to learn these techniques.

Notice how your voice is much lower in the morning, compared to after a stressful day at work. This is a result of physical tension in your jaw, facial muscles, shoulders and neck, which can contribute to voice strain. Relaxation exercises will help reduce this tension.

Humidity is crucial to the health of your voice. Install humidifiers in your home and work environments; sip water throughout the day. Cover your mouth in cold and dry environments, and breath through your nose. Smoking heavily and consuming a lot of alcohol can also permanently damage your voice.

Grammar and Sentence Structure

Besides tone, tempo and inflection, the structure of your sentences and the grammar you use are important to your image. Concentrate on speaking in full sentences. Your mind works much faster than your mouth, so it's understandable, although not excusable, when you speak in broken fragments. Speaking in full sentences gives you more time to process information, thus avoiding potential errors. As well, people will listen to you more carefully; you'll command more attention.

Listen carefully to good speakers and try to copy their techniques. Listening to books on tape, which are read by professionals, is another excellent way to hear good speaking skills.

The grammar and speech patterns that you use are reflections of your family culture and education. Grammar blunders will definitely be noticed by people who speak precisely. Inaccurate speech patterns are difficult, but not impossible, to modify. If this concerns you, contact a speech therapist, who can assess your situation and suggest a plan of action.

Maximize your potential:
Use a confident voice!

Chapter 19

Pregnancy Etiquette and the Workplace

You've just found out that you're pregnant. Now you must make a lot of decisions that will affect you, both personally and professionally. How and when will you announce your pregnancy at work? What sort of conduct toward a pregnant woman is considered inappropriate? What about maternity wear? Above all, how can you maintain your professionalism and plan for the future?

Announcing Your Pregnancy

When to Do It

There are differing opinions about when to announce your pregnancy to your immediate supervisor and co-workers. Some women want to tell everyone as soon as they discover the good news, others will announce it when they move into maternity clothes and a few feel that it's not necessary to say anything at all. At the very least, it's advisable to wait to announce your pregnancy until the second trimester, when miscarrying is less likely. However, each case needs to be examined individually to determine what is best.

There are many good reasons to make the announcement earlier rather than later. Perhaps your workplace handles hazardous chemicals that could be dangerous to the fetus; in case of an emergency related to your health, your employer needs to know about your condition early on. As your pregnancy progresses, the amount of time you'll need for medical appointments increases, and if you take the time during the work day, you'll need to give an explanation.

Knowing that you're pregnant may help your co-workers be more understanding if you're not feeling well. Your company may be going through a transition that involves reducing staff, and if they know that you'll be taking a leave of absence soon, they may reconsider the staff allocation. If you plan to take maternity leave, you must inform your Human Resources Manager eventually so that the necessary paperwork can be processed.

How to Do It

Before you tell your co-workers about your pregnancy, set up a meeting with your direct supervisor and discuss the situation. You could agree on time off for medical appointments, a reduced workload, a temporary transfer to another department or the timing and length of your maternity leave. Don't apologize for the fact that you may be inconveniencing your employer; simply deal with the matter straightforwardly.

Don't tell your co-workers before your supervisor because people can't keep secrets; the information is bound to leak out. When it's time to tell them, be sensitive. Some people may be dealing with fertility issues, have had a miscarriage or are childless for other reasons, so it may be difficult for them to share in your joy.

Maintaining Your Professional Image

Many changes take place during pregnancy, from the obvious physical and emotional demands to the challenges of managing your workload effectively and preparing for your leave. If you experience afternoon fatigue, switch your coffee break to a 15-minute cat nap to restore your energy and increase your productivity. Unless there's a medical reason, don't use your pregnancy as an excuse to avoid work. Maintain your usual working style as much as possible; separate your personal life from your professional role. This will help your supervisor adjust more easily to the organizational changes that will result from your pregnancy.

You'll need to plan for your maternity leave. Some employers may not hire a replacement, or they may reassign your duties at the last minute. It's best to be proactive and take ownership of the situation, especially if you'll be returning to your job. Begin to plan for your exit just as if you were organizing an educational leave. Make sure that your files are in order, a detailed job description exists and you're on top of any work in progress. If a medical emergency takes you away from your job much sooner than anticipated, the person who assumes your responsibilities will be grateful that you were prepared.

If you work in a high-stress environment, you need to consider not just long-term health but also your professional image. If the increased demands of pregnancy put your general health at risk, you may have to make some adjustments. Reducing your workload in the short term could actually have long-term benefits. Deciding early that it's advantageous to reduce your workload will enable you to find a replacement sooner for a smoother transition.

Technology also enables women to continue to work either part-time or full-time before and after the baby's birth. They can stay connected to colleagues and clients in their home office using teleconferences, computers, the Internet and e-mail.

Managing Inappropriate Behaviour

As soon you become pregnant, it seems that personal space and privacy are no longer important. Perfect strangers will come up to you and pat your abdomen. They may even apologize when they realize what they've done.

Since when does your abdomen become public property to be patted, poked and rubbed? If this bothers you, you can use humour and respond with: "Please don't wake the baby," or you can say something more direct, such as: "I don't appreciate you touching my stomach. I'm sure you understand."

Probing questions and rude comments like the examples below are also improper.

- "How much weight have you gained?" isn't fair at any time.
- "Wow! You're as huge as a whale!" or "You could put a pizza box on your stomach!" does nothing for a woman's positive frame of mind.
- People who ask: "How long have you been married?" could be working on the nine-month calculation or making an inappropriate value judgment about your marital status.
- "What does your husband do?" is equally invasive.
- Sexual innuendoes such as "Boy, you've been busy" are always out of line.

- One of the most frequently asked questions: "When are you due?" can also get people into trouble. Perhaps you've already delivered your baby and haven't yet shed the weight you gained during pregnancy. Or worse still, you might not be pregnant at all.
- "When are you going to have your next baby?" is no one's business but your own.
- Well-meaning people can also test your patience. Being asked: "How are you?" by every person that you meet can become tiring. Besides, they don't really want to hear about your backache and that you couldn't sleep because of heartburn.
- The epitome of redundancy is saying: "So, you haven't had the baby yet?" to someone who is obviously in her ninth month and can't wait for labour to begin.

During her pregnancy, a woman who worked in a smoke-filled bar regularly received this comment from customers: "You shouldn't be working here—it isn't healthy for the baby." She was aware of this, but jobs were hard to find, and she had to pay her rent.

You can handle most questions with humour. One woman I interviewed worked out regularly during her pregnancy in a gym. When someone exercising beside her said: "You look like you're fighting a losing battle," she retaliated with: "At least when I'm finished, I'll have something to show for it!"

Handling Paternity Leave and Adoptions

Paternity leave and adoptions must be managed with the same sensitivity and professionalism on both sides. If you decide to take paternity leave, people at work should support you in your decision to care for your child. You also need to prepare for your leave with the same care as mentioned above.

If you're applying for adoption, you need to tell your supervisor because you can suddenly become a parent overnight and need to take time off. Your co-workers should greet this addition to your family with the same enthusiasm as any new child. Probing questions about your fertility are obviously inappropriate.

Choosing Professional Maternity Clothing

When it comes to your maternity wardrobe, designers have thankfully come a long way from Peter Pan collars, frilly lace and tent dresses in large floral prints. Unless you have a romantic approach to clothing (as discussed in the chapter on wardrobe strategies), these styles will do nothing for your self-image, whether you're pregnant or not. The round lines used to create them will also make your body appear larger.

Some of your first purchases will be lingerie. It's true for all women that having well-fitting, supportive undergarments make you and your clothing look good. With the increase in weight that you experience during pregnancy, a maternity bra is essential. If you wear pantyhose, cutting the waist of regular-sized hose will get you through the first few months.

More stretch yarns are being used in clothing, so many women are choosing not to conceal, but to reveal, their changing body shapes. It's essential that you look like a working woman who is pregnant rather than a pregnant woman who is working. If you normally wear tailored, professional attire and leave the more body-revealing styles for your off-hours, do the same when you're pregnant.

Most women consider maternity wear expensive, especially when you can only wear garments for a few weeks before having to shop again. One reason that maternity clothing costs more is that you'll wear and wash it more often in a shorter period of time than any other clothing you own. To ensure that maternity wear can withstand this rigour and still look good, manufacturers must use quality fabrics that cost a bit more.

Purchasing regular plus-size clothing may work for the early months of your pregnancy, but as your waist continues to expand, you can't just go up a couple of more sizes. If a garment fits your abdomen, the area around your neck, armholes and shoulders will be too large. The fit guidelines covered in the chapter on establishing a quality image also apply to maternity wear.

When you begin to show, instead of trying to make do with your regular wardrobe, look for styles that have been designed with adjustable features, thus increasing the time that you can wear them. You can usually wear these pieces after your pregnancy. Also, some stores that sell infants' clothing and accessories rent or sell second-hand, professional maternity attire in excellent condition. And of course, most gently used clothing stores are also a source of maternity wear.

You'll often inherit maternity wear from well-meaning friends who've had their children just ahead of you. You may be lucky to find someone who has your taste in clothing, but chances are, the items that you receive don't suit your lifestyle and personality, require another piece to make them wearable, are too casual or are stained. (As your abdomen expands, it tends to brush against things and become permanently marked with substances like photocopying toner.) Many of these garments may be suitable only for your leisure time.

If you can't find your style or size range in the maternity department and your hand-me-downs are inappropriate for your workplace, work with an image consultant, designer or seamstress to create an integrated wardrobe capsule, in which the pieces mix and match to give you a multitude of options. The key is to start with basic garments in classic colours so that you won't quickly tire of them. (The chapter on planning your wardrobe will show you how to make 20 outfits from nine pieces of clothing.) Many women have found that a dark three-piece suit with a coordinating blouse is an excellent starting point. Fashionable maternity clothing that is suited to your personality and work environment is an investment in your well-being and professional image.

Maximize your potential:
Manage personal change professionally!

Chapter 20

Body Language

Dr. Mehrabian's study, described in the chapter on image management basics, noted that our face was responsible for 55 per cent of the impression people form of us when meeting us for the first time. Greeting a stranger with an open expression and a smile is instrumental in establishing an instant rapport. However, communication also involves your body language. The posture you adopt at a meeting, the way you carry yourself as you walk, folding your arms during an argument—all give visual clues to those observing you.

In his book, *Body Language: The essential secrets of non-verbal communication*, Julius Fast quotes Dr. Birdwhistell, professor of research in anthropology at Temple University, as saying: "No body position or movement, in and of itself, has a precise meaning" (Fast 1970, 118). Fast continues to explain, "In other words, we cannot always say that crossed arms mean, 'I will not let you in,' or that rubbing the nose with a finger means disapproval and steepling the fingers superiority . . . Sometimes [these impressions are] true, and sometimes they are not, but they are only true in the context of the entire behavior pattern of the person" (Fast 1970, 118). For instance, you may find it comfortable to cross your arms. However, if an argument ensues and you'd like to reconcile yourself with the other party, it may be advisable to unfold your arms in a gesture of peace and calmness.

When your body language contradicts your words, your credibility will be questioned. For example, if you say you're excited but are sitting slouched in a chair with an expression of boredom on your face, your mock enthusiasm will be abundantly clear.

When you're in a job interview or meeting a client for the first time, practise openness using body language. Maintain good eye contact, sit upright and be attentive. If you're nervous, avoid the tendency to twist your hair, play with your pen or fidget restlessly.

It's often advisable to mirror the posture of the person you're with. If they lean forward, it can be your invitation to follow. A slightly forward posture and occasionally nodding your head shows the speaker that you're interested in what he or she is saying. Be careful, however, not to punctuate every statement with a nod.

Be conscious of others' personal space. Acceptable distances will vary with each circumstance. Out of necessity, we tend to stand closer to a stranger in an elevator than we do in a large hotel lobby. Cultural differences also affect personal space, so if you're travelling abroad, investigate them beforehand.

If you need to gain the upper hand at a meeting, try sitting with your hands clasped behind your head with your arms above everyone else. Posture that is different from that of others can give you the advantage you need.

The way you organize your office furniture will allow people to approach you readily, or it'll keep them at a distance. If you want to appear non-confrontational and open in your business dealings, try moving from behind your desk and sitting beside your client at a round table.

Maximize your potential:
Use your words and body language consistently!

Chapter 21

Removing Communication Barriers from People with Disabilities

The world we live in includes people with disabilities. People often assume that someone who can't hear is unable to communicate. Even more hurtful is the opinion that because someone is hearing-impaired, they must have a mental disability. People who need to use a wheelchair for mobility can still make their own decisions and speak for themselves. People who have a visual impairment may appear confused when someone leaves them in the middle of the room without telling them where the furniture is placed. But this doesn't mean that they'll be confused when it comes to doing business.

To avoid uncomfortable, inappropriate or damaging situations, you need to gain an awareness of the disabilities with which some people live and, in certain situations, an understanding of unique forms of communication.

When you're faced with acquiring any new skill, it's best to learn from the experts. If you encounter a person with a disability, ask them if there is a particular avenue of communication that works better than another. Again, the worst thing you can do is make assumptions. Not all people with a hearing impairment can read lips. Before you act, inquire what is best for them.

Physical Impairment

The appearance of a person with a physical disability isn't necessarily different from that of an able-bodied person. To illustrate this point, I'll recount a personal experience. As a child, I contracted poliomyelitis, which left me with a few muscles paralyzed in my lower limbs. Most of my life, I've been able to walk with no visible signs of this physical disability. Upon occasion, though, I experience weakness and have to resort to using a cane. As a result, I obtained a special parking permit that enables me to park in the spaces designated for people with physical disabilities.

More than once, I've driven into a parking lot and parked in such a space. Before I've opened the door, people have honked and frantically pointed to the Handicapped symbol that marked the spot. Once, before I even set foot on the ground, the parking attendant came running across the lot, yelling and waving his hands in the air. Usually my response is to pick up my cane and wave it over my head like a standard leading me into battle. I've also been tempted to contort my face and body to live up to people's expectations. Why assume that a person with a physical disability wouldn't have a "normal" appearance?

The following are some helpful points for when you encounter a person with a physical disability:

- Don't assume that a person with a physical disability also has a mental disability.

- If a person in a wheelchair is travelling with an attendant, don't ignore the person in the chair and ask their attendant what the person wants. This often occurs in restaurants and retail stores.

- Ask people with physical disabilities if they need help. If they indicate that they do, ask how you may be of assistance; otherwise, you could cause them harm.

- Don't assume that people with disabilities can't complete activities unaided. Although it might take longer, they may prefer to be left alone.

- Don't assume that people with physical disabilities look different from those who are able-bodied.

Hearing Impairment

The following are common misconceptions that people hold about people with hearing impairments:

- **Deaf people can read lips.** Not all people with a hearing impairment can do this, and those who can communicate in this manner can't usually understand all the words.

- **Deaf people can't use the telephone.** Special teletypewriters (TTYs) are available. If you're talking with a person who uses a TTY, communicating may take a little longer.

- **People who have unusual-sounding speech patterns are mentally impaired.** This is false. The speech of most people who have hearing impairments is formed farther back in the throat and, consequently, sounds different.

• **All deaf people are mute.** People with hearing impairments have normal vocal chords. Not all have learned or choose to use them. People's quality of speech is better when they have some residual hearing.

• **Deaf people are referred to as *deaf mute* or *deaf and dumb*.** If it's necessary to refer to a person's hearing impairment, these are inappropriate terms. Today it's proper to use either *deaf, deafened* or *hard of hearing*. These terms are subject to change, and it's important to remain current. Your local hearing society will be able to help.

American Sign Language

Many deaf people use American Sign Language (ASL); it uses facial expressions and body language to communicate. Courses in ASL are available at continuing-education programs at high schools and colleges. Although most of the signs have the same meaning in the United States and Canada, some may differ; the following anecdote is an example.

A Canadian friend of mine once went to New York to visit a relative. She wanted a cup of tea and used ASL to ask for it. Her host pointed to the staircase that led upstairs. My friend asked again, this time signing carefully and with more insistence. Her host gave her the same response. After two more attempts, my friend spelled out the word: T-E-A. Her host burst out laughing. The Canadian sign for tea was the same sign that in New York meant *toilet*!

Preparing the Environment

When you communicate directly with a person with a hearing

impairment, you must prepare the communication environment.

- Reduce background noise.
- Sit or stand as close as is comfortable.
- Face the person squarely.
- Use good lighting.

Preparing Yourself

You'll communicate most effectively with the other person by preparing yourself as well.

- Before talking, get the attention of the other person. A slight movement of your hand is all that is necessary to catch the person's eye.

- Position yourself near their better ear. If the person is wearing a hearing aid, position yourself near the ear with the device. A hearing aid often helps the person hear sounds, but it doesn't always provide the means for sounds to be understood.

- Don't obstruct the view of your face with your hands or make unnecessary movements by chewing, smoking, etc. Don't look down or away while you talk.

- Speak in a natural voice and enunciate clearly; don't exaggerate your lip movements or speak too quickly or too loudly.

- If an interpreter is present, don't face the interpreter; continue to face and talk to the deaf person.

- Avoid excessive use of drugs or alcohol, which will alter the sound and formation of your words, distorting your communication.

- Use appropriate facial expressions and body gestures to add information to your speech. If you're not used to doing this, it may feel uncomfortable or exaggerated at first, but ultimately, it will help communication.

- Use short, simple sentences. If the person doesn't understand you, try changing your words and phrases or use a pen and paper.

- When the topic of conversation is about to change, let the other person know.

- Relax and be patient to keep communication channels open.

Acquired Hearing Loss in Seniors

You might find it helpful to know that about 50 per cent of people over 65 years of age have some form of hearing loss. Because they've usually acquired this loss gradually, their speech patterns may be the same as a person who isn't hard of hearing. As a result, you may not realize that to be understood, you need to speak to them clearly and slowly.

Visual Impairment

As with any situation, individuals will react to blindness or visual impairment in unique ways. Understanding the following points may help you communicate effectively with someone who has a visual impairment. Again, when in doubt, ask if and how you can be of assistance.

Making Contact

Approach a blind person and initiate the greeting using a normal tone of voice. Identify yourself and ask if the person wants your assistance. If they do, touch your hand to the back of the person's hand as a signal for them to take your arm. Don't grab their arm and pull them forward.

Crossing the Street

Avoid pulling the blind person by the hand or arm. It's awkward and confusing. Offer your assistance, and they'll tell you what is the best way to guide them. Let them know when you're coming to a curb and whether you'll be stepping up or down.

Orienting the Person

Describe the surroundings of an unfamiliar setting: the layout of a room, whether it's square or narrow, how many tables and chairs there are and how they're arranged. When you're travelling, talk about the landscape, the direction you're going and the names of towns as you pass by. Don't say "over there"; instead, give clear and accurate directions.

Using Language

Don't hesitate to use normal words such as "see," "look" and "read." For example, "Let's see what is on the menu."

Approaching Doorways

Inform the person that you're approaching a door and in which direction it opens. For example: "The door opens on the left, with the hinge side towards us." If the door is on a blind person's side, don't cross their path to open the door. The person who opens the door is responsible for holding it open until you both pass through.

Approaching Stairs

Alert the person when they're about to walk up or down stairs. Approach the stairs squarely and tell the person whether they're curved. Come to a full stop at the stairs, then go up or down one step ahead. The blind person will take hold of the railing and find the first step by sliding one foot forward until they detect the edge. Stop at the end of stairs and say, "Last step."

Sitting Down

When you're helping a blind person sit down, bring them into contact with the front of the chair so that their knees lightly touch the seat. Tell the person what type of seat is in front of them: armchair, bench, rocker, etc. If you're approaching the chair from behind, put the person's hand on the back of the chair.

Additional Tips

- Push chairs under the table when you get up.
- Keep doors entirely opened or closed.
- Keep cupboard doors closed.
- When you approach irregularities in the ground—for example, stepping from concrete to grass—alert the blind person in advance.
- If the person is with a guide dog, they may or may not want assistance. Remember that when the guide dog is in harness, it's working. Don't approach or pet the dog.
- When you leave a blind person alone in a room, let them know. If possible, ensure that you leave the person touching an object for reference, such as a chair or sofa.

Additional Strategies for People with Disabilities

It's common knowledge that people make immediate assumptions about others they meet for the first time, and people with physical disabilities probably experience more negative judgments than those who are able-bodied. To help counteract this, you can take advantage of these additional image management strategies.

- If you have a physical impairment that causes you to walk with a noticeable limp or sway, consider using a mobility aid such as a cane. Not only will your posture be more upright, thus making you more powerful, you'll probably have more energy.

- If you're visually impaired and often wear clothing that is mismatched, ask a sighted person to help you organize your closet. There are simple techniques that you can adopt to identify pieces that coordinate. For example, you can use safety pins that will go through the wash; this is especially good for pairing socks. You can also use pins to mark a soiled area so that you can pay closer attention to it when you launder the garment.

- If you're hard of hearing and wear a hearing aid that you don't want people to notice, consider purchasing one of the smaller models that fit into the ear canal (if that type is suitable for your hearing loss). You can work with a hairstylist to camouflage it.

- You can also have fun with decorative covers for behind-the-ear hearing aids. You can wear lightening bolts, bananas or jewelled fish over the mechanical apparatus and make a strong fashion statement.

- Work with an image consultant to ensure that you always

appear appropriately dressed and groomed for every situation. This person can also help you organize your wardrobe into useful modules, as outlined in the chapter on planning your wardrobe.

Maximize your potential:
Look beyond disabilities and focus on the person!

Chapter 22

Dining Protocol

Never underestimate the importance of dining protocol to your image potential; a large percentage of restaurant meals are business-related. A surprising number of adults admit to not knowing which fork to use or where their bread-and-butter plate is located. Because the busy schedules families keep mean that meals are eaten on the run, teaching dining etiquette in the home is rare today. However, futures can be successfully decided or negatively terminated during a business luncheon or dinner. With deals being made over meals, dining protocol is an essential image management skill for any business professional.

There is something about the dining table that makes it a proving ground for prospective employees and potential suppliers of goods and services. For example, being asked to lunch has become a very important part of the job interview. If you salt your food before tasting it, an employer may think you have an impulsive nature. Shoving food into your mouth can be a sign of aggressive behaviour. Being indecisive over the menu doesn't bode well if you're applying for a position in which you're expected to make independent, quick decisions.

The white tablecloth and its accompanying tableware can be a bewildering battlefield if you're not equipped with an accurate map. Dining protocol can provide you with the strategies you need to turn the tables in your favour. Your polite behaviour at the table will signal a certain sensitivity and leadership potential that people will remember.

The very nature of dining with someone is an intimate situation; this is because you're sitting close to each other at the table. No one can escape being seen; all eyes are watching. Similarly, the knee-crushing seating arrangements of some airplanes require a certain finesse and protocol when you eat to avoid jabbing your fellow passengers and making a long flight even longer.

However, with education, experience and trial and error, you can learn to handle yourself while eating in professional and social situations. You'll learn what to do about that escaping olive rolling across the white linen tablecloth in your superior's direction. You'll be able to deal with the catapulting fork that was in your capable hand just seconds ago. And the spilled glass of red wine, coursing across what was once a pristine surface, will no longer be such a threat.

Table manners are more often about how we react to these inevitable disasters than how we act when everything is running smoothly. A sure test of character and politeness is being able to deal with these incidents with the appropriate ease and grace. A firm grasp of basic dining protocol will help you confidently mop up after the pitfalls that you'll inevitably encounter during your life and career.

Please Take Your Seats

When it's time to take your place at the table, here are some essential dining protocol pointers.

• At a large, formal dinner of more than eight people, place cards usually indicate where you'll sit. In a very large gathering, you're given a table number, and the seating plan (normally at the door) will help you find your seat. At very formal dinners, couples aren't seated together; if round tables are used, couples can be seated at separate tables.

• In less formal gatherings, your host[1] will direct you to your seat. Couples do sit together.

• Men and women are usually seated alternately around the table, but it's not required, especially if there is more of one group than the other. The guests of honour are seated to the right of the hosts. With a gathering of eight at a rectangular table, one guest of honour may be seated at one end of the table to maintain the male/female seating pattern, or two of one gender may be seated together.

• At a formal meal, don't take an unfinished drink from the cocktail hour to the table. In an informal setting, the host will usually encourage you to bring your drink to the table.

• If your purse is small, place it on your lap; otherwise, put it on the floor under your chair with the strap out of the way of the wait staff. If you're carrying a briefcase or portfolio that is too large to fit under your chair, place it upright close to the side of your chair. Don't put cellular phones or pagers on the table.

---

1. Throughout this book, the term *host* refers to both men and women.

Setting the Stage

The table setting is both logical and efficient. Flatware is placed nearest the hand that will be holding it, and because most people are right-handed, glasses are on the right.

Flatware Is Placed Strategically

The number of pieces of flatware at a place setting is determine by how many courses there are and what is on the menu.

- In the Continental style of eating, you usually hold your fork in your left hand and your knife in your right, so forks are set to the left of the dinner plate and knives to the right. The exception to this is the seafood fork, a small fork used for eating shellfish, which is placed on the right. (For more on the Continental style, see "Continental" later in this chapter.)

- No more than three of one type of utensil are set at one time. If a fourth fork is required for dessert, it's brought in just before serving or with the dessert. The more formal the dinner, the greater the number of utensils there will be in the setting.

- For a formal meal that consists of rolls, shrimp cocktail, soup, fish, main meat or vegetarian course, salad and dessert, the flatware is arranged like this:

  - The salad fork is next to the dinner plate on the left.
  - The dinner fork is to the left of the salad fork.
  - The fish fork is to the left of the dinner fork.
  - The salad knife is next to the dinner plate on the

Dining Protocol: Setting the Stage

right with the cutting edge turned inward.

• The dinner knife is to the right of the salad knife.

• The fish knife is to the right of the dinner knife.

• The soup spoon is to the right of the fish knife.

• The oyster fork is to the right of the soup spoon.

• The dessert fork and spoon are placed horizontally above the plate; the spoon is on top with the handle to the right, and the fork is below the spoon with the handle to the left.

• The butter knife is laid horizontally across the bread-and-butter plate with the curved edge down.

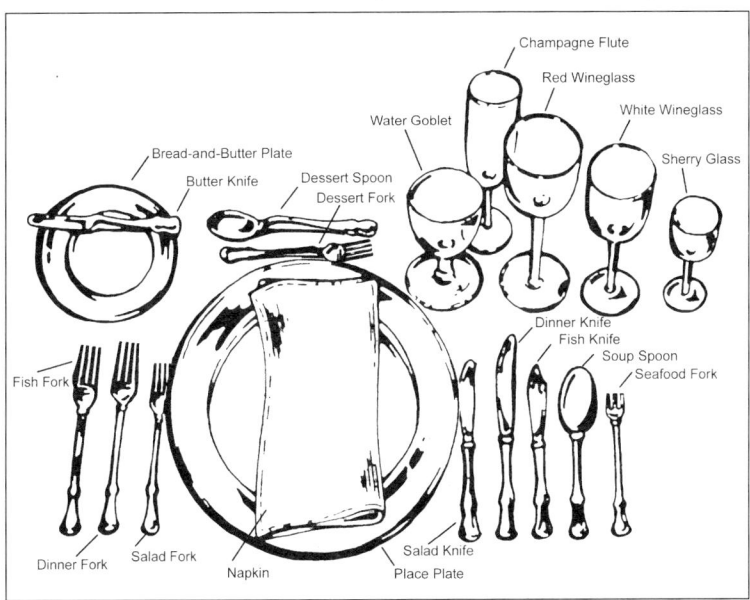

This table is set for a six-course meal consisting of shrimp cocktail, soup, fish appetizer, main course, salad and dessert. The first three courses are served on the place plate, which is then removed.

From Outside to Inside

Begin eating with the utensils that are on the outside left and/or right and move to the inside. When in doubt, follow your host. If there is no host, keep your eye on someone at the table who appears confident. If you're to be the host, everyone will be expecting you to take the lead.

Solids on the Left, Liquids on the Right

Like flatware, the number of side plates is determined by what is on the menu, and the number of glasses depends on how many beverages and courses will be served.

- When salad is being served at the table, the salad plate is set immediately to the left of the place setting. The bread-and-butter plate is placed above it.

- When salad is being served from the kitchen and brought out on individual plates, if there is room on the table, the bread-and-butter plate is placed to the immediate left of the forks. The salad is placed in front of you and is removed once you're finished.

- Glasses for water, wine and sherry are placed above your knives. The order of the glasses can vary according to size and when you'll use them. Traditionally, the water glass is first, followed to the right by the red wine, white wine and sherry glasses. The champagne flute is placed above these glasses because champagne is served with dessert or used for toasts at the end of the meal.

- The red wineglass has a larger bowl and is usually taller than the white wineglass. The larger surface area of the red wine in the glass allows the bouquet, or fragrance of the wine, to escape more readily and be enjoyed.

• The smaller bowl of the white wineglass holds less and is therefore refilled more often. This helps to keep the wine, which is usually served chilled, from becoming too warm.

Centre Stage

In a formal dining room, your place is set with a plate, larger than a dinner plate, called a *charger* or a *place plate*. Your appetizer and/or soup plates are placed on the place plate, and it's removed before the main course is served.

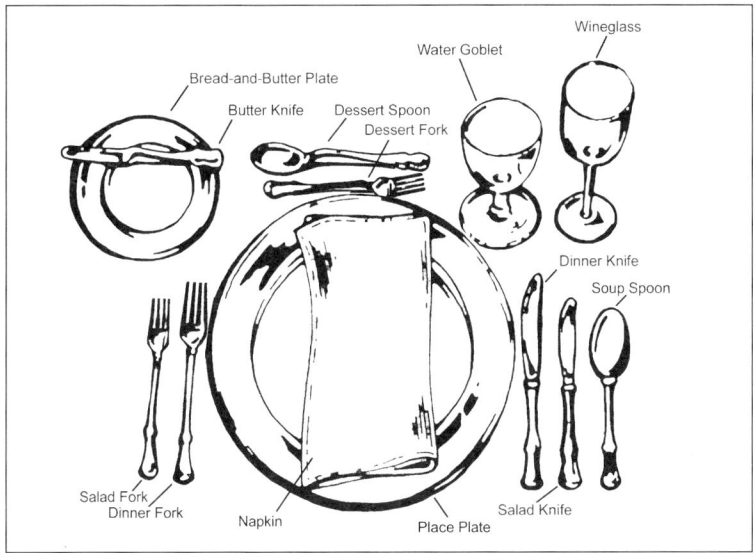

The four-course menu for this table setting includes soup, salad, main course and dessert.

Napkin Nuances

There is a certain protocol for unfolding and using your napkin.

• At a hosted dinner party, wait until the host places the napkin on his or her lap before you do so.

- Unfold your napkin without snapping it in the air. Leave a large dinner napkin (55 to 75 cm, or 22 to 30 inches) folded in half and place it on your lap with the crease towards you. Open luncheon napkins (35 to 60 cm, or 14 to 24 inches) entirely.

- Don't tuck your napkin into your belt, shirt or collar.

- Use your napkin frequently to blot or pat your lips; don't wipe your mouth vigorously.

- If you need to be excused from the table during the meal, fold your napkin in half and place it on your chair. If other people are still eating, it's unappetizing for them to see a soiled napkin on the table. If your napkin isn't soiled, you may place it on the table to the left of your plate; however, the wait staff may take this as a sign that you're finished your meal and remove your plate.

- When you've finished your meal, don't fold your napkin back into its original format. Pick it up by the centre or casually fold it so that it's not too bulky. Then place it either to the left of your dessert plate, if it's still on the table, or if it's been removed, in the middle of your place setting.

Let the Dining Begin!

The moment when you may begin eating depends on the format of the meal.

- **Dinner party:** When the host is served and picks up their fork to begin.

- **Round table of six to ten:** When everyone has been served.

- **Buffet**: When you've gone through the line and sat back down, it's considered courteous to wait for one other person to join you.

- **Large dinner party:** The host will encourage guests to begin after two or three people have been served so that they can eat their meals while their food is still hot.

Table Conduct

Once you sit down to your meal, here are some pointers for how to conduct yourself.

- If a utensil appears soiled, don't wipe it on your napkin. Politely ask for a clean one.

- It used to be that only your wrists were allowed on the table during the meal. (This is still true in some countries outside North America.) It's now permissible to place your elbows on the table if it's between courses and dishes have been removed, or if you haven't ordered food for a particular course and you're waiting for the others. However, your dining companions may not know of this recent change in protocol and may think that you're being impolite. Consequently, it may be prudent not to place your elbows on the table at any time.

- Sit up straight. Don't tip back in your chair, slouch, lean your arm on the table or put your arm around your plate.

- When you eat, open your mouth just as you bring your food to your mouth. Don't leave your arm resting on the edge of the table and lower your head to your food.

- Don't play with the utensils on the table while you wait

for others to finish. Use your utensils quietly. Don't punctuate the conversation by stabbing the air with your fork.

- Never place soiled utensils on the table.

- Cut your food with your elbows close to your body.

- Take modest bites so that your face isn't distorted; eat everything on your spoon or fork with one bite.

- Don't talk with your mouth full.

- Eat quietly with your mouth closed. Don't eat too fast; pace yourself to finish your meal at about the same time as your dining companions.

- Dab your mouth and fingers often with your napkin.

- Don't ask for a second helping. If there isn't enough food to go around, you'll embarrass your host.

- To eat the last of the sauce on your plate, you may use a piece of bread on your fork. Never pick up the bread in your fingers and wipe up what remains on your plate.

- If you're served food you dislike, don't complain. Push it around your plate and converse with your dinner companions.

- Don't touch anything from your shoulders up with your hands (except for using your napkin properly, of course). If your nose needs attention, you may take out a handkerchief and quietly wipe it. If you need to blow your nose, leave the table.

- If the space around the table is crowded, move slightly from side to side to enable the wait staff to serve you properly.

- Pick up items only if they're within easy reach. If you'd otherwise need to reach across the table or stand to reach them, ask for them to be passed to you.

- If you need to leave the table during the meal to go to the washroom, wait for an appropriate time, such as between courses, then excuse yourself, place your napkin on your chair and return quickly. It's not considered polite to leave the table to have a cigarette, make a phone call or speak to someone else in the dining room.

- Don't lift your plate from the table and hold it under your chin to prevent crumbs or sauce from falling on your lap. Leave the plate on the table and, with a straight back, lean over the plate to ensure that any crumbs land on the plate.

Passing and Adding

There is a certain protocol to passing food and serving yourself.

- Food is usually passed to the right.

- Don't serve yourself community food (sugar, salt, pepper, salad dressing, bread) until you first offer it to someone else.

- Always pass the salt and pepper as a pair; pass a pepper grinder separately.

- Serve yourself modest amounts of food, sauces and gravies.

- Don't add salt and pepper or sauces to food before tasting it. In a fine restaurant or in someone's home, it's rude to ask for a sauce.

Grasping the Glass

Depending on the contents of your glass, it needs to be handled in a certain way.

- Hold long-stemmed glasses for water and wine by placing your thumb and first two fingers at the base of the bowl. If wine is chilled, hold the glass by the stem just below the bowl so that you don't change the temperature.

- Hold short-stemmed glasses by the stem.

- Pick up tumblers near the base.

- Hold brandy snifters in the palms of both hands to warm the brandy.

- Hold cups with handles by inserting your index finger through the handle. Your thumb should be just above the handle for support, with the second finger below it for added security. Don't elevate your little finger in an affected manner, and don't ignore the handle and place your entire hand around the cup.

- It's safer for everyone to leave their glasses and cups on the table when they're being filled.

- If you don't want to have wine, gesture to the wait staff with your hand and say, "No, thank you." Don't turn the glass upside down or place your hand firmly over the opening.

Implementing the Essentials

There are certain recommended ways to hold and use your utensils to cut and eat your food.

Get a Grip on It!

Here are guidelines for holding cutlery properly. While they're written for people who are right-handed, people who eat with their left hand can reverse the directions.

When you eat with one utensil:

> • Hold the utensil like a pen, grasping the fork or spoon with your thumb and forefinger about three-quarters of the way up the handle. Your other three fingers are underneath, with the weight of the utensil resting on your middle finger. Press your thumb down from the top for added security. *Never grasp the handle with a fist from the top.*

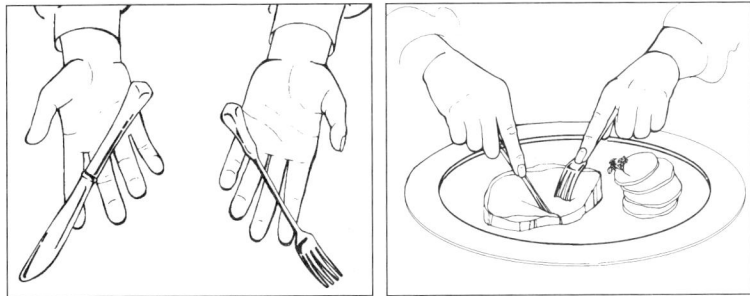

Holding utensils

When you use two utensils to eat or cut food:

> • Pick up your knife so that the end of the handle sits at the crease where your smallest finger joins your hand. Place the tip of your first finger where the handle meets the blade and with the blade facing the tips of your fingers.

> • Grasp the handle of your knife with your second, third and fourth fingers, then turn your hand over.

- Place your first finger on the top edge of the knife blade just above the handle. By bearing down on this finger, you can cut the toughest piece of food easily.

- Place the fork with the tines up in your left hand in the same manner as the knife. To maintain good control, place your first finger on the back of the fork below the tines but just above where the handle begins. Apply pressure with both your thumb and forefinger.

- The ends of the handles of both utensils should be hidden inside your hands.

Cutting Remarks

When you cut your food, do it with finesse.

- Don't cut your complete dinner into bite-sized pieces at the beginning of the meal. Cut one or two pieces at a time.

- Draw the knife toward you; don't saw back and forth. If the food is tough, request a steak knife.

- Never hold the fork perpendicular to the plate in a fist-like death grip.

Choosing Your Eating Styles

There are two general ways of handling your utensils: the *American* and the *Continental*. Dorothea Johnson, in her volume *The Little Book of Etiquette*, gives some historical information on these two styles.

> "Until the 1840s Americans and Europeans ate in the same style—with the fork in the right hand. In the mid-nineteenth century, however, the fashionable upper

class stopped shifting their forks back and forth between their right and left hands. As more middle-class eaters learned to convey food into their mouth with tines instead of blades, the upper class hit upon this as a new class identification. It became fashionable first in England. Then in 1853 a French etiquette book described the latest mode of dining favored by fashionable people. Before long, all Europeans began eating in this style." (Johnson 1997, 38-39)

Both styles are acceptable in North America; however, the Continental is often preferred in formal settings in Britain. By mastering both methods, you can switch at will to the style that is best suited to your meal and possibly being used by the majority of people at the table. Use the style that is most comfortable and practical for you, depending on the type of food you're eating and the company you're with.

American

The American style of eating uses the knife and fork to cut food, then puts the knife down and uses the fork to eat.

• When you're eating with one utensil, hold the fork in your right hand, as described in "Get a Grip on It!" earlier in this chapter.

• If you need to cut something, move the fork to your left hand, pick up the knife in your right hand and hold them as described in "Get a Grip on It!" when eating with two utensils.

- After cutting a bite-sized piece of food, remove the morsel from your fork with your knife. Put your knife across the top of your plate on the right, transfer your fork to your right hand, then pick up your food with your fork and guide it to your mouth.

- Use your knife as a pusher to guide food onto the tines of your fork. You can also use a piece of bread, but if you're concerned that it may seem less graceful, avoid doing it.

Continental

The Continental style of eating uses both the knife and the fork during the entire meal.

- As I described in "Get a Grip on It!" earlier in this chapter, hold your fork in your left hand, with the tines down, and the knife in your right.

- Once you cut a morsel, either pierce it with your fork or use your knife to push it onto the back of your fork (which has its tines down). Then with the tines of your fork still down, transfer your food to your mouth. (Some people brought up with strict manners in English homes and boarding schools have had to eat peas this way. Either they speared each pea with their fork, or they balanced six peas on the back of their fork and put them in their mouth without mishap; pushing them onto a mound of mashed potatoes on their fork wasn't an option.)

Positioning

It's important to realize that the way you position your utensils gives a signal to the wait staff.

Pausing

Positioning utensils in this manner indicates to the wait staff that you're pausing during your meal.

• Rest both utensils across your plate. Place your knife so that the handle is at the lower right of your plate and the tip of the blade is in the centre with the cutting edge turned toward you. Place your fork, tines down, in the equivalent position at the lower left of your plate.

• Place your spoon on the plate beneath your cup, bowl or compote. Don't leave it inside, sticking out.

• Place your butter knife horizontally across the top of your bread-and-butter plate with the curved edge down.

• In an informal restaurant where you've received only one fork and knife for two courses, don't move the utensils to your bread-and-butter plate between courses. Allow the staff to sort out this dilemma. They may move the utensils to the bread-and-butter plate for you or remove them entirely and bring clean ones for the next course. Staff who haven't been properly trained will place them on the table.

• Remember, if you need to be excused from the table during the meal, fold your napkin in half and place it on your chair.

Finishing

Positioning your utensils this way signals the wait staff that you're finished eating.

• Place your knife on the right of your plate going diagonally, as when you're pausing. Place your fork below and parallel to the knife, with the tines up or down. It's somewhat safer with the tines up because the fork will be more stable when the plate is removed.

• If you excuse yourself from the table before finishing and inadvertently place your cutlery in this way, you may find your food gone when you return.

• When you've finished your soup, place your spoon on the plate beneath your cup, bowl or compote.

• Never pile your bread-and-butter plate on top of your dinner plate or stack other people's plates to make it easier for the wait staff.

• Don't hand the wait staff plates, cups or utensils when the course or meal is finished unless the seating is so crowded that they can't reach your place setting safely.

• At a formal dinner, if your host places their napkin beside their dinner plate and rises, dinner is over.

• See "Napkin Nuances" earlier in this chapter for notes on how to place your napkin when you're finished a meal.

Rolling along Smoothly

When the meal includes a basket of bread or rolls, here is how you politely partake.

- Sometimes there is no host to get the basket of rolls moving. If the basket is within easy reach, pick it up, open the linen cover, then hold onto the basket firmly and offer it to the person on your left. Then choose a roll yourself and pass the basket to the person on your right, who'll take a roll and pass the basket to their right. Should the first person wrestle the basket from you, let it proceed to the left.

- Place the roll on the plate to your left. If there are two plates, the smaller one above and to the left of your dinner plate is the bread-and-butter plate. The other one, which is slightly larger and is to the left of your dinner plate, is the salad plate. If there is no bread-and-butter plate, place the roll on the edge of your dinner plate or on the tablecloth to your left.

- If a butter ball or pat isn't already on your bread-and-butter plate, take one from the dish with the special fork provided. If the butter is in one large piece, use the serving knife that accompanies the butter dish to transfer a modest amount of butter to your bread-and-butter plate.

- Don't use the butter-serving knife to butter your roll; instead, use your own butter knife to butter each piece as you eat it. If no butter knife has been provided, use your dinner knife. Never use your soiled dinner knife to take butter from the butter plate. If there is no alternative, wipe your dinner knife on your roll first to remove any traces of your dinner.

- Don't cut your roll in half with your knife. And don't butter the whole roll before you begin to eat it! Pull each bite-sized piece from the roll and butter it on your bread-and-butter plate just before you eat it.

- If bread is served instead of rolls, take one slice at a time and either handle it as you would a roll or break the slice of bread in half and butter each half just before you eat it. Don't hold the whole slice of bread in two hands and lower your head to eat it (like corn on the cob at a picnic.)

Soup's On!

Soup can be especially tricky to eat politely. Following these guidelines, however, you'll carry off this course with aplomb.

- Spoon the soup away from you.

- Don't blow on hot soup. Instead, make conversation with your dining partner until the soup is cooler, then spoon near the edges of the bowl.

- In a formal setting, don't break up crackers and put them in your soup. Don't dunk your roll either.

- Soup spoons are usually too large to fit completely into your mouth. Sip soup from the side of the spoon without making a slurping noise.

- When only a small amount of soup remains in your bowl, slightly tip the bowl *away from you* and spoon only one or two times.

- If you pause during eating, place your spoon on the service plate beneath the bowl. Do the same when you're finished.

- Clear soups are sometimes served in a two-handled soup bowl. First eat any garnish with your spoon. When the soup is cool enough to drink safely, it's permissible to pick up the bowl by the handles with both hands. If you don't feel comfortable doing this, use your spoon. When in doubt, follow the lead of your host.

Let Us Eat Salad

In North America, salad is usually served after the soup and before the main course, whereas in Europe, it comes after the main course, often accompanied by cheese. When salad is served after the meal, it's usually with cheese and crackers; you eat it with a salad fork and luncheon knife.

- If there is a large amount of dressing on the salad, be careful because it can easily splash you or your dinner partners.

- If a salad fork is provided, use it instead of your dinner fork.

- If the salad is served as a vegetable on your dinner plate, eat it with your dinner fork.

- Either cut unmanageable pieces of lettuce with your fork and knife, or make little packets by folding the large pieces several times.

- If lettuce falls off your plate, put it back on the edge of your plate using your knife and fork and continue eating the rest of your salad.

Dealing with Dinnertime Dilemmas

- Dead or alive, a bug may lurk in your salad. If it's alive, pick it up with your napkin and don't call attention to it; if it continues to wander, you may need to squash it. If it's dead, hide it under a piece of lettuce and remember not to visit that site again. In a formal setting, don't mention it to the others at the table because it would make them uncomfortable and embarrass the host. In an informal restaurant setting with close friends, you may draw it to the attention to the wait staff, who'll usually replace your meal or adjust your bill.

• If food gets caught in your teeth, don't pick your teeth, even with a toothpick. Drink water to try to dislodge the offending morsel. If that isn't successful, excuse yourself from the table and remove the food in the washroom. If you're wearing braces, beware of long strands of cooked onions, pasta, etc.; it can be embarrassing when one end becomes lodged in your braces and you swallow the other, creating a tendency to gag.

• If you spill something on the table in a restaurant, apologize to your dinner partners. The wait staff will take care of it, usually by placing a napkin over the spot to avoid distraction for the rest of the meal.

• If you spill something on the table in someone's home, apologize and offer to help clean it up.

• If you spill a small amount of food on yourself, remove it with a clean knife or spoon, wrap your napkin around your finger, dip it in your water glass and dab the area. If the amount of food is too large to be handled this way, or if you're drawing unwanted attention, excuse yourself from the table and deal with it in the washroom.

- If you lose control of a utensil and it falls to the tablecloth, apologize to your dining partner, pick it up and continue eating. If it falls to the floor, ask the wait staff for another one.

- If you encounter gristle, bones or inedible bits while you're eating, don't spit them into your napkin or onto your plate. Bring your fork to your mouth and remove the offending morsel, then place it on your plate, where you can bury it.

- When a relish plate with olives and pickles is passed around, take a small amount and place it on your salad plate to the left of your dinner plate. As you eat the olives, place the pits back on your salad plate. If olives are part of the main course, place the pits back on the dinner plate.

- If an olive escapes and rolls across the table onto the floor, don't go after it. If it stays on the table within easy reach, apologize to your dining partner. Pick the olive up, place it off to one side of your plate and choose another one.

- When squeezing fresh lemon over your food, pick up the lemon wedge, push the tines of your fork into the middle of the cut side and squeeze the ends together. The fork ensures that the lemon doesn't slip out of your fingers, and it also helps direct the flow of the juice toward your food.

- If you've placed extremely hot soup or food in your mouth, don't spit it out. Quickly take a sip of cold water to cool your palette.

- In an informal setting, with the permission of your host and using only one hand, you may pick up chicken or meat by the bone to eat the remaining morsels that eluded you using your knife and fork.

• If you break something in a private home, first sincerely apologize, then offer to replace it. An added courtesy that your host will appreciate is to send a written note of apology accompanied by the replaced item. If the item is irreplaceable, send a gift of equal value and level of taste.

Dynamic Dessert Duo

The easiest way to eat many desserts is the Continental style-using two utensils, a fork and a spoon. In strict British homes, the spoon is always held in the right hand; otherwise, choose the best utensil for the dessert that you're eating, as outlined here.

• **Pie or cake à la mode:** With your fork in your right hand, use your spoon to separate a mouthful and guide the food to your fork.

• **Cut-up fruit and berries:** Eat these with your spoon in your right hand and your fork in your left.

• **Watermelon:** In a formal setting, eat this with a knife and fork. Use the utensils to remove the seeds first. If some seeds do enter your mouth, remove them with your fingers and place them on your plate. Do the same with grape seeds. However, it's better to avoid eating these foods in a formal setting altogether.

• **Ice cream, sherbet, sorbet, parfaits and puddings:** Use only your spoon. Near the end, tip the bowl away from you. (See "Soup's On!" earlier in this chapter.)

Licence for Lip Balm and Lipstick

Avoid being too liberal with these.

> • Be careful not to apply too much lipstick before a meal. You'll leave an obvious and unsightly residue on the flatware, glasses and cups, and you may stain the napkins.

> • Just as it's impolite to comb your hair at the table, don't apply lip balm or lipstick or touch up your makeup at the table. Use the washroom to freshen up.

Special Dietary Needs

Many people have special dietary needs that result from food allergies, medical conditions, lifestyle choices and cultural and religious restrictions. If you're the host, you need to be aware of these issues and broach the subject with each guest. If you're the guest, it's important that you let the host know what your needs are well in advance of the dining event. This will prevent embarrassment, awkwardness and perhaps, in the case of food allergies, a life-threatening situation. Contacting the host before the event will allow them to arrange menu alternatives and accommodate your needs seamlessly.

Vegetarianism is a growing trend in our society. If you're planning a meal for vegetarian guests, a few definitions will help guide you.

> • **Lacto-ovo-vegetarians:** Eat eggs, dairy products and vegetables. They don't eat meat, fish or seafood.

> • **Lacto-vegetarians:** Don't consume eggs or meat, but they do eat dairy products and vegetables.

- **Vegans:** Consume only plant-based foods such as whole grains, legumes, vegetables and fruits.

If you're unsure about a guest's dietary needs, ask specific questions. It's also helpful to make a list of the ingredients you used in the meal available to your guests should they need to know.

Dining Emergencies

Emergencies during a meal aren't likely, but sometimes they do occur. Here are some guidelines for dealing with an emergency that faces you or someone else.

- If you begin to choke on some food, or if you have an allergic reaction, it's imperative that you make at least one other person at the table aware of your dilemma. If the situation isn't life-threatening, and if you can, get up from the table with this person and make your way to the washroom. If your life is in danger, don't be concerned about protocol because time is of the essence. Make it known to the other person to call an ambulance. Many restaurants provide training for their staff in administering the Heimlich manoeuvre, which usually dislodges trapped food.

- If you're at a table with someone who begins to choke on their food, offer to help. If their life is in danger, summon the restaurant staff in a loud voice to call an ambulance. If you know the Heimlich manoeuvre, apply it immediately or ensure that the wait staff does.

- In most quality restaurants, the kitchen staff has been trained to safely prepare food for people with allergies. If you have extreme food allergies, make the wait staff aware of this so that they can take the proper precautions.

Maximize your potential:
Your future can be decided over a meal!

Chapter 23

Business Mixers and Cocktails

Most business dinners begin with a formal cocktail gathering or an informal happy hour. Despite the differences in formality, both are very similar. They're social occasions usually fraught with much activity, and this sets the tone for the evening to follow. You can use this important hour before the main event to your best advantage by practising good etiquette.

Business mixers are also prime opportunities to network with new people or people you've met briefly before and now want to develop a rapport with. It's important to be friendly at these occasions. If the thought of entering a room full of strangers sends a chill up your spine, the following ten tips will help you navigate such gatherings with friendliness and strategic sparkle.

Ten Tips on How to Work a Room

1. Accept That Nervousness Is Natural

At a young age, your parents taught you not to talk to strangers. So entering a room filled with people you don't know is uncomfortable. You need to redefine the "strangers" you're about to meet. If you look at the situation realistically, you'll recognize that there is probably a common thread that has brought you together. At a business mixer, you can assume that everyone there is interested in further developing their business. At a wedding, the common bond is knowing either the bride or the groom. With this awareness, the people you're about to meet aren't so strange after all.

2. Be Prepared

Come prepared to talk about three to five timely topics you've read about in newspapers, magazines and trade publications. Current events, human-interest stories, sports, theatre and movies are far more interesting than the weather. Bring a good supply of business cards and a pen.

If you don't really feel like attending a function, or if you don't think it'll be worthwhile, thinking positively will put you in a confident frame of mind. For example, instead of saying to yourself, "I don't like meeting people, and I'd rather be home watching TV," try: "I know I'm going to enjoy meeting some incredible people this evening, and they're going to find *me* fascinating." So that you don't congregate with those you already know, set a goal to meet three to five new people.

3. Eat before You Go

If you've skipped breakfast and lunch, you'll be hungry when you arrive at the event. Naturally, the buffet table will have a magnetic pull, and instead of meeting new people, the food will become the centre of your attention. Remember why you're there—to make new contacts, not to eat dinner.

4. Dress Appropriately, but with Impact

Carefully plan your clothing strategy. The colour, style and fabric of what you wear can create either a powerful or an approachable effect. If the dress is business casual, be careful not to bottom out. Remember that your professional image is tied to the minute details. What impact do you want to make? How are you going to make it?

5. Make a Deliberate Entrance

If you're nervous, it mustn't show. Don't slink into the room and cower in a corner. With your head held high, walk into the room with a sense of purpose. Take a few unflustered seconds to survey the room, then follow your instincts about whom to approach.

6. Never Approach a Group of Two

To achieve your goal of meeting new people, avoid the tendency to gravitate to people you already know. If you approach two people, you may be interrupting a private conversation; a person on their own, however, will be forever grateful if you walk up to them and introduce yourself. Failing that, choose a group of three or more people who aren't huddled together.

7. Become the Host and Break the Ice

In a business-mixer environment, don't wait for a proper introduction. It's better to be open and break the ice with a simple "Hello" than to be silent and miss an opportunity. Use a seven-second introduction that you've rehearsed beforehand. Extend your hand and give a firm handshake. Be a host, and introduce the person you've just met to either people you know or others whom you're meeting for the first time.

8. Master Small Talk

Engaging in small talk with someone about subjects you have in common isn't shallow because it opens the door for more meaningful conversation. If conversing with strangers doesn't come easily, the stress of making conversation will disappear when you concentrate on asking others about themselves. People always enjoy talking about their work, interests and concerns while you play the role of the attentive listener. The topics you prepared before the event will help get things going. Avoid sensitive subjects, listen more than you speak and ask open-ended questions. A skilled conversationalist will always manage to realign the focus in their direction when they need to.

9. Focus on Contacts, Not Contracts

Your goal should be to make meaningful contacts, not close deals. In order for people to give you referrals, they must know you, understand what you do and like you. It's difficult to reach this point in the short time that a cocktail party or mixer affords. If you think that the person you're talking to can help your career, or if you believe that you have valuable contacts for them, ask them if you can call to continue the conversation. After the event, make notes on the back of the business cards you've received and follow them up immediately.

10. Break Away Graciously and Continue to Network

It's important to break away and continue meeting people. Summarize your conversation with the person, lean away, say, "I look forward to seeing you again," smile and walk a third of the room away.

If for some reason this seems rude, ask the person if they'd like to meet other business professionals, and take them along with you.

Attending Private Cocktail Parties

If the cocktail hour, open house or business mixer is taking place in a private home or club, remember the following:

- For an event scheduled from 5:00 p.m. to 7:00 p.m., you can arrive up until 5:30 and leave no earlier than 6:30. Don't stay past 7:00.

- Modulate your voice to fit the space. Have fun, but don't bellow!

- Admire, but don't handle, the host's *objets d'art* unless you've been given permission.

- Don't wander through the house unless your host gives you permission.

Handling Liquid Refreshments

Liquid refreshments, alcoholic or not, create their own challenges. Here are some tips for handling drinks.

- Drink responsibly in all circumstances. If you're jet-lagged, fatigued or need to get up early the next morning, mocktails may be your best choice. A company or other business event isn't the place to let your guard down; many promotions have been reconsidered the morning after.

- Beer drinkers beware! It's more than acceptable to pop a cool one and drink from the bottle at your local pub or on the deck, but not at a formal cocktail party or business-related happy hour. Use a glass.

- To avoid greeting others with a cold and clammy hand, hold your drink in one hand, reserving the other for handshakes.

- Make sure that you use coasters for your drink to protect fine furniture. If your host doesn't provide a coaster, don't hesitate to ask for one. It shows that you care and pay attention to detail.

- Don't leave your glass unattended. It's your responsibility, and in a home where there is a crowd, the brush of a cuff can spell disaster.

Juggling Hors d'oeuvre and Canapés

As I mentioned in "Ten Tips on How to Work a Room" earlier in this chapter, it's best to eat before you attend a cocktail party so you're not entirely focused on the food. It's acceptable to nibble, but not to gorge. The following tips will help you juggle drinks and food while working the room.

No cocktail party would feel right without the delicate balance of a drink, hors d'oeuvre, napkin and, of course, the elaborate choreography that must accompany this jumble of items as you attempt to circulate through the crowd. This pivotal hour, where ice jingles, glasses clink and small objects of food often fly from your hand in defiance of gravity, can be the most trying of all etiquette challenges.

This needn't be the case if you remember a few pointers. If the cocktail party is business-related, it's crucial that you keep this in mind: Your focus is on doing business while making a good impression.

- Learn the finesse of holding your napkin, plate and glass in one hand so that you can access any of them at will—and still have a hand free to shake hands.

- Take only one or two pieces of food at a time; it's impolite to load up.

- At a catered function, never ask for more hors d'oeuvre—it's the wait staff's responsibility to circulate the room as required. In a private home without wait staff, it's the host's responsibility to ask you if you'd like another smoked oyster.

- Before you take anything else from the serving tray, make sure that you take a napkin. Be vigilant so that your hands are clean and not dripping lobster mayonnaise or salsa. Sticky digits aren't welcome!

- If you don't have a plate, toothpicks spearing layered delights create a special challenge. After you've consumed the tidbit, you're left with a splinter of a problem. For health reasons, *never* place a used toothpick on a serving tray or platter. Most considerate hosts and caterers will leave ample receptacles around in which to deposit these things. If not, it's acceptable to place used picks in ashtrays or in your napkin. Before you sit down for dinner, dispose of your cache by leaving the napkin with your glass on a tray provided by the wait staff for this purpose.

Devouring the Morsels

The aesthetic qualities of well-designed cocktail delicacies can only be eclipsed by their being seemingly eater-unfriendly. Here is a brief guide for eating them politely.

- Beware of hot hors d'oeuvre that have a reputation for maintaining an internal temperature that exceeds that of an overly microwaved hot dog. Before putting something in your mouth, carefully sample the temperature by touching it gingerly to your lips and then to the tip of your tongue.

- Raw vegetables and dip require a bit of finesse in using your napkin and hand-eye-mouth coordination. Select the vegetable of your choice, then dip it carefully into the sauce; at the same time, position your cocktail napkin under the delectable and hold it there until you've successfully transferred it to your mouth. You won't drip anything on you or the carpet.

- Puff pastry conceals another hazard because it has a bad habit of squeezing out its contents and splashing innocent bystanders. Make sure it's cool first, and if size allows, subtly pop it whole into your mouth. If in doubt, hold your napkin under your mouth to catch any contents that may escape.

- There may be times when your culinary curiosity is piqued to the limit and you'll try an hors d'oeuvre that tastes horrible. When this happens, excuse yourself, turn your back to the people you're with, transfer the offending morsel to your napkin and look for a place to dispose of it. If turning away from your companions isn't polite, quickly swallow the morsel before it has a chance to permanently taint your taste buds.

Maximize your potential:
Approach business mixers with confidence!

Chapter 24

Dining Conversation

With the details of dining protocol in place, you can now turn your attention to dining conversation, which has almost become a dying art in our fast-paced life. Beyond avoiding contentious topics such as religion, politics and morality, there are other strategies to consider.

When you dine in a large group, it's polite to engage in conversation with people who are within easy hearing range. Avoid talking to only one person throughout the meal, and be careful not to monopolize the conversation. In a noisy environment, where you can only talk with one person at a time, converse with the person on your right for the first course, and then turn your attention to the person sitting to your left for the next course.

In a social setting or at a long business dinner, don't sit down and immediately start talking about business. It's annoying, and other people at the table may judge you as being too aggressive or boring or as harbouring a self-seeking agenda. Others may question your awareness of the world around you and your sensitivity to your dining partners, especially if some people present aren't in the same business.

Similarly, when a business meal is arranged, don't ignore the signs to begin discussing business and make small talk throughout the meal. You'll be remembered as superfluous, unresponsive and a time-waster.

Turning the Conversation to Business

In business entertaining, the role of conversation and the point at which business should be discussed varies with the situation. If you're the host, begin by asking your dining partners if they're under any time constraints. (You should have stated the purpose of the meal at the time that you arranged it so that everyone could come prepared.) The time allotted for the meal is an excellent guide to the appropriate time at which business can be discussed. Remember that it's your responsibility as host to guide the conversation at all times. (The role of the host at business functions is discussed more thoroughly in the chapter on hosting large business functions.)

During Breakfast

At a 45-minute breakfast, there isn't much time to talk. Once the first cup of coffee has been served, the conversation can immediately turn to business.

During Lunch

At an hour-long lunch, where no outside people are present and there is a problem to solve, the business discussion should start after the food orders are taken. If outside guests are present, ten minutes of small talk while the food is being ordered is sufficient. If you're the host, look for a logical point in the conversation and lead into the business discussion. If it's difficult to do this, try using humour to make the transition: "Well, now that we've settled the entire future of the Mudville Sentinels, let's get down to business."

During Dinner

A dinner is much longer than a business lunch, so move into serious discussion after about a half-hour of socializing. This relaxed break from the day's activities will help revive tired minds. People who need time to refresh and regroup may not welcome moving into business topics too quickly; they may also not be as productive.

Maximize your potential:
Resuscitate the dying art of conversation!

Chapter 25

Business Lunches and Dinners

There will be many times when you'll be required to go to lunch with business colleagues, clients and your boss. You may have occasion to host a more formal business lunch or attend one as a guest. Whether you are the host or the guest, make sure you know how to handle these situations and project a professional image.

Hosting a Business Lunch

The business lunch is a fundamental part of doing business. You can make a favourable impression on a business associate or potential client by hosting a business lunch with great flare. In addition to knowing which fork to use, where to place your napkin and a myriad of other essential details of dining protocol, following some basic guidelines will ensure that everything runs smoothly.

Arranging the Lunch

Organizing all the details of the lunch well beforehand will show courtesy to your guest and ensure that the lunch goes smoothly.

• Invite your colleague to lunch at least three days to a week ahead of time.

• Give them a choice of two restaurants that you think would be suitable. (For example, a vegetarian wouldn't appreciate a steak house, a less agile person may have difficulty sitting on the floor in a Japanese restaurant, *nouvelle cuisine* might not be appropriate for an athlete in training and a family-style restaurant might not be the best choice for someone who entertains with refined elegance.)

• If you're from out of town and you know people in the city, ask them to suggest some restaurants. If it's feasible, investigate them before inviting your guest.

• If the restaurant is very formal, check to see whether it's permissible to bring out business papers at the table.

• Make reservations in your name and company name.

• If you have important business matters to discuss, ask for a private table; a table near the kitchen or front door can be distracting.

• If you're a smoker and smoking is allowed in the restaurant, consider whether your guest is a smoker or non-smoker. If they're not, refrain from smoking and sit in the non-smoking area.

• The day before the lunch, reconfirm your reservation and call your guest to remind them of the lunch. Don't ask them if they're still coming; instead, ask if the time is still appropriate and tell them how much you're looking forward to the lunch.

Before Your Guest Arrives

Attending to a few last-minute details will set the tone for lunch.

- Arrive at the restaurant 20 minutes early to ensure that you're there before your guest and that the table is suitable.

- If something unexpected occurs and you'll be a few minutes late, let the restaurant know. Ask the maître d' to explain this to your guest when they arrive and to serve them a drink.

- To avoid having the bill come to the table, give your credit card to the maître d' and ask them to add the appropriate amount of tip.

- Don't touch anything on the table while you wait for your guest to arrive.

- If your guest doesn't arrive within 20 minutes of the agreed-upon time, call them.

- If you can't reach your guest after 30 minutes has gone by, either order your lunch or leave the restaurant. If you choose to leave, give the server a generous tip.

During Lunch

During lunch, being generous with ordering your meals, and knowing proper dining protocol, will put you both at ease.

- When your guest arrives, stand up and shake hands.

- If you and your guest walk in together, let your guest walk ahead of you to the table. Have your guest sit in the best seat, preferably facing the room. If you have more than one guest, seat the guest of honour on your right.

- Ask your guest to order first. If you've eaten at the restaurant before, make one or two suggestions such as: "I really enjoyed the filet mignon the last time I was here" or "Red snapper is in season. If you like fish, the chef has a delicious way of preparing it." After comments like these, your guest won't feel obliged to order an inexpensive item.

- If your guest orders a drink, order one for yourself. If your guest orders an alcoholic beverage, you may join them or order a soft drink if you prefer; you don't need to offer an explanation. If you do order something alcoholic, exercise caution; it's important that you maintain your professionalism, both during and after the meal.

- If your guest orders soup, an appetizer, or dessert, do likewise.

- Avoid ordering foods that are difficult to eat such as whole shrimp, lobster in the shell, spaghetti, and French onion soup. The effort and skill you need to eat these gracefully will be better spent discussing business.

- After ordering lunch, conversation can turn to business unless your discussion involves paperwork. In this case, wait until after the meal, when the table has been cleared.

- Don't complain about the food, the restaurant or the wait staff. If your guest has concerns, deal with them promptly.

- Don't pick up dropped items from the floor. Ask the wait staff to help.

- Use proper dining etiquette when you eat, remembering that you're the host and that you'll need to lead the way. (Check the chapter on dining protocol for more details.)

- Ask your guest if they require anything; if so, politely ask the wait staff for their assistance.

- If your guest eats more slowly than you normally do, pace yourself accordingly. Be aware of your guest's schedule and help bring the meal to a close on time.

Handling the Bill

At the end of the meal, handle the bill quickly and discreetly.

- As host, you're expected to pay the bill, with no contribution from your guest(s).

- If you haven't given your credit card to the maître d' before the lunch, quickly check the bill and deal with it discreetly.

- If there is an error on the bill, speak to the server after your guest has left.

After the Lunch

Courtesy and good manners apply after lunch too. Attend to the final details and solidify that good impression.

- Escort your guest to the door and thank them for coming. If you've used the coat check, tip the attendant for both coats.

- Thank the maître d' for the good service and leave them a tip.

- Follow up any business issues discussed and thank your guest if they've been helpful in any way. Writing a note is always best. Many business associates now use e-mail, which isn't as effective as writing but much better than forgetting to thank them altogether.

Being a Polite Guest

When you're a guest yourself, extend the same politeness to your host.

- Arrive on time.

- Order a mid-priced meal.

- Thank the host for the meal in a day or so.

- If you want to continue the business relationship, after the lunch, make a note in your calendar to return the invitation in a month's time.

Being Interviewed at Meals

It's not uncommon for a business meal to be part of a job interview. Make sure that your behaviour makes, not breaks, your chances of success.

- Don't take a long time deciding what to order. Some job interviewers have been known to decide against a candidate based on the lengthy time the interviewee spent pondering the menu.

- Don't order the lowest—or the highest-priced items on the menu.

- Don't season your food before tasting it; some interviewers will judge you as an unsuitable, rash decision-maker.

- Order food that is easy to eat so that you can concentrate on the interview.

- Don't order alcohol; you could lose the job if the company has a policy against alcohol consumption at business meals. Besides, you need to keep your mind as clear as possible.

- Brush up on your dining protocol before you go to the interview.

Lunching with Colleagues

While going out to lunch with colleagues is a less formal type of business lunch, a certain protocol still applies.

- Never invite your boss for lunch. This rule may be stretched if you're part of company management or you've worked with your boss for a long time and have a very close relationship. When in doubt, stick to the rules.

- When you first join a company, you may want to invite your peers out for lunch to get to know them and the company. Space such meals out over time so as not to appear overeager.

- If your boss invites you to lunch, he or she pays. Otherwise, whoever extends a lunch invitation, regardless of gender, pays the bill. If someone is unaware of this protocol and seems to want you to contribute, gracefully offer to pay half.

- When several employees of the same company go out to lunch together, you each pay for your own meal unless your boss has extended the invitation.

- Always thank your boss or business associate for treating you to lunch.

Other Business-Related Meals

Other business-related meals require you to know how to handle the situation: going-away and birthday lunches and attending dinner parties.

Going-Away and Birthday Lunches

Make certain that these occasions are happy ones by being sure what to do.

- When a lunch is arranged to mark a special occasion such as a birthday, the one who's being honoured isn't expected to pay.

- If the meal takes longer than your usual lunchtime, offer to work through your breaks to make up for the lost time.

Dinner Parties

Because they're social occasions with an overtone of business, dinner parties raise a number of different questions.

- When your boss invites you to their home, it's considered a social occasion. You may return the invitation if you wish and invite them to your home.

- If a business associate invites you to a social occasion, the invitation should be addressed to both you and your partner before you can assume that your partner can attend. If you're unsure, ask politely for clarification. If you're asked, remember to R.S.V.P. promptly.

- When you're doing business entertaining with a spouse, your spouse should participate fully and make your guests feel welcome. For example, they should greet your guests at the door, join in the conversation and assist with refreshments.

• Don't focus your conversation on children or domestic affairs.

Maximize your potential:
Master business lunch and dinner protocol!

Chapter 26

Hosting Large Business Functions

You may at times be asked to host a large business function. Many company or company-sponsored events require a host: corporate conventions, training seminars, product launches, community charity events and retirement celebrations. Because of their size and to make sure that they're properly organized and run smoothly, these important business events need a host. A good host not only ensures that corporate events come off successfully but also enhances the corporate image inside and outside the company.

Taking on the role of host is a big responsibility. While it may seem daunting at first, it provides an excellent opportunity to show off your leadership skills. Being an effective host at a large business function is a skill you acquire like any other—with observation, research and experience. There are four elements that will ensure that you'll be a good host in any large business or social situation: thoughtful respect for others, a warm and engaging attitude, an eye for detail and a thorough understanding of good manners.

Before the Event

Depending on the size of the event, you may be the sole person organizing it, or you may be the chair of a committee that has been formed for this purpose. In either case, it's important to be organized and to delegate responsibilities to other people if necessary.

- Determine how invitations are to be extended (for example, by telephone, in writing, inter-office memo, e-mail, company publication, etc.). Make sure that the invitations are sent out well in advance; if necessary, set up a system to record the replies.

- Make sure you understand the purpose of the function. Its goal will affect your planning. A public charity event sponsored by your company will have different requirements than a company business mixer.

- Determine whether any guests have special dietary or beverage needs and make provisions for them with the caterer. Dietary needs can range from health-related concerns to cultural and religious dietary restrictions. A good host will be as accommodating as possible in this area.

- If it's required, or if it's company policy, arrange transportation to and from the event.

- Liaise with guest speakers, special guests, the master of ceremonies, entertainers, etc. to make sure that they're informed of all the arrangements, that they know their respective roles and that you are aware of any specific needs they might have.

- The role of a host can be very demanding. At a large, complex event, you may not have time to eat. Plan to eat before the event begins.

- Introduce yourself to the head of the wait staff or to the dining room supervisor and make yourself available to them if they have any questions or concerns.

- Arrive well in advance. This ensures that you're available to answer any questions, review last-minute arrangements and greet early arrivals.

During the Event

During the event, you'll want to make sure that things run smoothly and your guests enjoy themselves.

- Position yourself at the entrance to the event to welcome your guests. If many guests are attending, you may need to have several greeters. At a formal sit-down function, ensure that all guests know where they're sitting; using table numbers and a simple seating plan will help.

- Be mindful of time constraints and adhere to a schedule. Make sure that the cocktail hour doesn't extend into the time when dinner will be served. You may consider closing the bar at a specific time to encourage your guests to take their seats.

- At catered functions, be sure to position yourself at a table in view of the service door. This enables you to monitor the wait staff, give directions and ensure that every table is served.

- At smaller events, the role of the host is focused on one individual. As host, you're responsible for the comfort and enjoyment of your guests. Involve all the guests at the table in the festivities and conversation. Introduce everyone to each other and make sure that the conversation flows. It's essential that no one is isolated.

- Larger business functions may need table hosts. Like the single host at a smaller event, they welcome the guests to their table and make sure that they enjoy themselves.

There are many duties that a host must perform, and they vary, depending on the size and complexity of the business occasion. Carry them out to the best of your ability, but remember that what is important is to have a genuine concern for your guests. This will make up for any details that you may miss because of inexperience. Sincerity is valued over knowledge in most etiquette situations, and people will react positively to it. Acting as a host is an excellent opportunity to show off your wide range of leadership skills and make your professional image shine.

Maximize your potential:
A good host is a good leader!

Works Cited

Armour, Stephanie. 2000. Companies rethink casual clothes: Dressing down brings slacking off, some CEOs say. *USA TODAY*, 27 June.

Fast, Julius. 1970. *Body Language: The essential secrets of non-verbal communication.* New York: MFJ Books.

Johnson, Dorothea. 1997. *The Little Book of Etiquette.* Philadelphia: Running Press.

Keers, Paul. 1988. *A Gentleman's Wardrobe: Classic Clothes and the Modern Man.* New York: Harmony Books.

Mehrabian, Albert. 1981. *Silent Messages: Implicit Communication of Emotions and Attitudes.* Belmont: Wadsworth Publishing Company, Inc.

Richards, Dan. 1999. The Two-Minute rule. *Forum*, January/February, 9–12.

Spillane, Mary. 1993. *Presenting Yourself: A Personal Image Guide for Women.* London: Judy Piatkus.

Temple, Linda E., and Karen R. Loewen. 1993. Perceptions of Power: First Impressions of a Woman Wearing a Jacket. *Perceptual and Motor Skills*, 76, 339–348.

Yaqub, Reshma Memon. 1995. Getting It Right: The Latest Angle on Etiquette and Protocol. *The Washington Post*, 16 January.

Zezima, Jerry. 1995. Gut-wrenching ache puts squeeze on men. *The Toronto Star*, 28 January.